California Bar Examination

Essay Questions and Selected Answers

July 2014

The State Bar Of California
Committee of Bar Examiners/Office of Admissions

180 Howard Street • San Francisco, CA 94105-1639 • (415) 538-2300
845 S. Figueroa Street • Los Angeles, CA 90017-2515 • (213) 765-1500

ESSAY QUESTIONS AND SELECTED ANSWERS

JULY 2014

CALIFORNIA BAR EXAMINATION

This publication contains the six essay questions from the July 2014 California Bar Examination and two selected answers for each question.

The answers were assigned high grades and were written by applicants who passed the examination after one read. The answers were produced as submitted by the applicant, except that minor corrections in spelling and punctuation were made for ease in reading. They are reproduced here with the consent of the authors.

Question Number	Subject
1.	Contracts/Remedies
2.	Evidence
3.	Business Associations / Professional Responsibility
4.	Criminal Law and Procedure
5.	Trusts / Community Property
6.	Torts

ESSAY EXAMINATION INSTRUCTIONS

Your answer should demonstrate your ability to analyze the facts in the question, to tell the difference between material facts and immaterial facts, and to discern the points of law and fact upon which the case turns. Your answer should show that you know and understand the pertinent principles and theories of law, their qualifications and limitations, and their relationships to each other.

Your answer should evidence your ability to apply the law to the given facts and to reason in a logical, lawyer-like manner from the premises you adopt to a sound conclusion. Do not merely show that you remember legal principles. Instead, try to demonstrate your proficiency in using and applying them.

If your answer contains only a statement of your conclusions, you will receive little credit. State fully the reasons that support your conclusions, and discuss all points thoroughly.

Your answer should be complete, but you should not volunteer information or discuss legal doctrines that are not pertinent to the solution of the problem.

Unless a question expressly asks you to use California law, you should answer according to legal theories and principles of general application.

Question 1

Percy and Daria entered into a valid written contract for Percy to design and install landscaping for an exclusive housing development that Daria owned. Percy agreed to perform the work for $15,000, payable upon completion. Percy estimated that he would work approximately 100 hours a month on the project and would complete the project in three months. His usual hourly fee was $100, but he agreed to reduce his fee because Daria agreed to let him photograph the entire landscaping project for an article he planned to propose to *Beautiful Yards and Gardens* magazine. He anticipated that publicity from the article would more than compensate him for his reduced fee.

Percy completed two months' work on the project when Daria unjustifiably repudiated the contract. He secured a different project with Stuart in the third month, which paid him $1,500 and took 15 hours to complete. He could have completed Daria's project at the same time.

At the time Daria unjustifiably repudiated the contract, Percy was negotiating with Tammy to landscape her property for $30,000. Once Tammy learned what had happened, she stopped negotiation.

Percy has sued Daria. Ideally, he would like to finish the project with her.

What remedy or remedies may Percy reasonably seek and what is the likely outcome? Discuss.

QUESTION 1: SELECTED ANSWER A

Contract Law - Common Law

In contract law, the common law governs service contracts or land sale contracts, and the UCC governs the sale of goods. This is relevant because there are certain differences in remedies between the two areas of law, and certain remedies that are specific to the UCC.

This was a service contract, because Percy was to perform the service of landscaping the yard. Therefore, the common law and its remedies apply, which will be discussed below.

Breach Of Contract and a Valid Contract

A breach of contract claim requires there be 1) a valid contract, 2) a breach, and 3) damages. The problem says they entered a valid written contract, so there is no issue there.

Breach - Anticipatory Repudiation

Anticipatory repudiation occurs when a party clearly and unequivocally communicates or manifests that it will not perform its duties on the contract. When there is an anticipatory repudiation, the other party may treat the repudiation as a breach or ignore it and demand performance until the original performance was due. When one party has entirely performed before the agreed upon date, and the other party repudiates by refusing to pay - i.e. the only duty remaining is for one party to pay - the non-breaching party may not sue for damages until the original agreed upon date.

Here, Daria clearly manifested that she would not pay, and the problem says it was unjustifiable. Percy can take this as a breach of the contract. Also, Percy had not completed performance and so there are more duties due than simply one party paying.

Therefore, Percy may bring a breach of contract claim for any resulting damages, discussed below.

Monetary Damages

The general and presumed damages in contract law are monetary damages, with seek to compensate the non-breaching party with money. In certain situations, which will be discussed below, equitable remedies such as specific performance will be granted. But the default is damages, so these will be discussed first.

Expectation Damages

The default contract remedy is expectations damages. Expectation damages seek to place the non-breaching party in the same position he or she would have been in had the breaching party performed. Said another way, expectation damages seek to give the non-breaching party the benefit of its initial bargain. The general formula for expectation damages is the difference amount of price or the amount to be paid for a service or good under the contract and the amount of replacing (the market price) it, plus any incidental damages, plus any foreseeable consequential damages, less any amount saved by the non-breaching party.

Here, the general damages to which Percy would be entitled include the amount of money he stood to earn under the contract ($15,000) less the amount he could get paid for replacement work. There is a tricky issue regarding the magazine spread in Beautiful Yards and Gardens, because Percy can possibly argue that the value of that was at least $15,000, and so his total expectation was $30,000, and therefore if the court does not grant specific performance (see below), it should award him expectation damages of $30,000 minus any replacement services he provides and any amount he saves. This is because Percy would have completed 300 total hours of work (100 hours a month X 3 months) and he would normally charge $100 for each hour (300 X 100 = $30,000). Daria might argue that he only expected to make $15,000 and so that should be the amount from which to measure Percy's expectation damages.

Because the initial contract amount was only for $15,000, Daria has a strong argument that that amount was the only amount Percy could reasonably have expected to make. In the event the specific performance is not granted, and therefore Percy does not get the added publicity, it will be difficult for him to claim he expected to earn more than $15,000 and so arguing for his traditional hourly rate will probably fail. If he wants to collect more in the absence of specific performance, he could possibly argue under a restitution theory.

Consequential Damages: Lost Contract with Tammy

Consequential damages are damages that are unique to an individual party (i.e. they are not those that are clearly within the contract, such as the contract price) but that are the natural and foreseeable consequences of a contract breach or are contemplated by the parties when contracting. Importantly, to collect consequential damages, the damages must be proven with reasonable certainty and they must be foreseeable.

Here, Percy will argue that his lost contract with Tammy was a consequence of Daria repudiating their contract, and therefore the consequential damages of that $30,000 contract should be included in his damages with Daria. He will point to the timing, and that he and Tammy were negotiating a deal but Tammy stopped upon learning that Percy's contract with Daria ended. Percy might argue that Tammy stopped negotiating because the broken contract with Daria gave Tammy reservations about contracting with Percy.

Percy's consequential damages argument is subject to many counter-arguments by Daria, which will probably win out.

Causation of Breach

First, there is a causation issue. Daria can convincingly argue there is no proof that her repudiation even caused Tammy to stop negotiating. Therefore, it might not even be a "consequence" of her repudiation and should not be included in Percy's damages claim.

Certainty

Tammy can argue that there is no certain amount of the consequential damages with Tammy. They were negotiating over a price of $30,000, but that was not the final, agreed upon price, which could have been less. Further, there might not have been a contract at all. Therefore, there is no reasonable certainty that but for Daria's repudiation, Percy would have earned $30,000 from Tammy.

Foreseeability

Lastly, even if Daria's repudiation caused Tammy to cease negotiating, Daria can argue it was not a natural and foreseeable consequence of her repudiation, nor did Daria contemplate such a consequence when entering the contract. Daria repudiated the contract unilaterally. She never alleged that Percy was doing a bad job, and she has done nothing further to impugn his business reputation. While it is arguably foreseeable that someone canceling a contract might make the other party look bad, it is likely not a natural consequence of one individual's repudiation to cause another party to back out of a contract.

Disposition

Percy should not be able to collect consequential damages from the lost deal with Tammy in his claims against Daria.

Incidental Damages

Incidental damages are naturally arising damages that a party occurs when trying to fix the situation after another party breaches. Incidental damages include costs such as trying to renegotiate other deals. Here, it is unclear any specific incidental damages Percy may collect, but he will be able to collect any that do exist.

Mitigation and contract with Stuart

A non-breaching party has a duty to mitigate damages by seeking reasonable replacements or substitutes for goods or services. Thus, in his third month on the job, Percy had a duty to mitigate by finding replacement work. Any damages Percy collects from Daria must be reduced by what Percy earns from these mitigating contracts, and if he does not mitigate, the law will treat Percy as if he did and not allow him to collect if there were reasonable replacements for his contract with Daria.

Here, Percy entered into a contract with Stuart to complete 15 hours of work for $1500 in the third month. Daria will argue that this was mitigation and therefore that any damages he collects from her should be reduced by this amount as adequate cover.

Lost-Volume Seller

A party does not need to reduce expectation damages by the cost of cover or replacement performance if the party is a lost-volume seller. Generally, this applies to sellers of goods who have enough supplies to meet the demands of their customers, such that the other party breaching does not just allow the seller to sell to a new party, but the breaching party merely constitutes a lost sale the seller could have met anyways. If a party is a lost volume seller, cover or replacement service will not reduce its damages.

Here, Percy was not a seller of goods, but he could have performed the contract for Daria and the contract for Stuart. Thus, the contract for Stuart makes Percy look like a lost volume seller because he could've performed both and thus could've made the $15,000 from Daria and the $1500 from Stuart. Therefore, the $1500 from Stuart should not count as mitigation and should not reduce any damages he collects from Daria.

Other Mitigation

There are no specific facts about seeking cover, but the fact he negotiated a deal with Stuart and was attempting to enter a deal with Tammy suggests he was looking for adequate replacements. Thus, Percy has met his duty to mitigate and his damages from Daria should not be reduced.

<u>Disposition of Expectation Damages</u>

He is entitled to the $15,000 regardless of specific performance (see below) because he expected to make that, but not the lost contract with Tammy and not reduced by the contract with Stuart. This should be increased by incidental damages and decreased by any amount he saves by not having to further perform. If he does not get specific performance, he might recover extra in restitutionary damages for the benefit conferred on Daria (See below).

Reliance

Reliance damages seek to place the non-breaching party in the position he or she would have been in if the party had never entered into a contract. Thus, reliance damages generally consist of reasonable expenses the non-breaching party has incurred in preparing and partially performing the contract.

Here, there are no clear reliance damages amounts, but Percy could collect any amounts he's spent on tools specifically for Daria or other related expenses.

However, these are likely to be less than the $15,000 expectation damages, and a party may not collect both expectation and reliance damages, so Percy will likely not try and collect these damages.

Restitution

Restitutionary damages seek to compensate the non-breaching party for benefits he has conferred on the breaching party in order to prevent unjust enrichment by the breaching party. In some circumstances a breaching party may even be able to collect restitutionary damages if he has substantially performed and thus conferred a substantial benefit on the other party. Restitutionary damages may take the form of either the amount of improvement the breaching party has enjoyed, or the value of the services provided by the non-breaching party. Courts have equitable power to choose one or the other, and will consider factors such as the blameworthiness of the parties.

Here, Percy has performed 2 months of work at 200 hours total and thus the market value of his benefit conferred upon Daria was $20,000. Percy will argue he should at least get paid this if he cannot finish the contract. This is more than the $15,000 in expectation damages, but it is arguably fairer if he doesn't get specific performance because this is the value he conferred on her. Daria might argue that he did not substantially perform because he only completed 2/3 of the work, but Percy was not a breaching party, and so he is not blameworthy and therefore he needn't substantially perform to seek restitution.

If the amount of increased value of her land is even higher, Percy might argue for that, but such a number is unclear from these facts. Because he's conferred $20,000 worth of services and thus benefited Daria to that amount, Percy can argue for this amount as well instead of expectation damages if he wants. If he gets specific performance and finishes and the original contract is enforced, he would not get restitution damages because the other remedies would suffice.

No Punitive Damages

Even though Daria's breach was intentional and without justification, punitive damages are not award for breach of contract claims, and therefore Percy may not collect any.

Specific Performance

It is within a court's equitable powers to grant specific performance as a remedy in certain circumstances. Specific performance requires that both parties actually complete the contract, rather than compensate each other in money for any breach. Specific performance requires 1) a valid contract, 2) with clear provisions that can be enforced, 3) an inadequate legal remedy (i.e. money damages are insufficient for some reason, such as the good or service is unique), 4) balancing the hardships, performance is equitable, and 5) enforcing the performance is feasible.

Valid contract with clear terms

The contract was valid and the terms were clear as the payment and services were unambiguous.

Inadequate legal remedies

Percy will claim that mere expectation or restitutionary damages are insufficient because he entered the contract thinking he would be able to photograph it and get more publicity to further his business. Specifically, he will claim that it is difficult to value the worth of this increased publicity and therefore it cannot be remedied with mere dollars and can only be remedied by allowing him to finish performance.

Daria can argue that he can be compensated for his time adequately by paying him his normal hourly rate, and that he can always just photograph another project of his. This is a close issue. If Daria's yard would've been particularly nice or a particularly good display of Percy's work, then maybe this performance was unique. If it was any ordinary yard, then absent a showing that Percy needed to place the advertisement now, legal remedies should suffice and Percy could just photograph another project.

Equitable

In terms of balancing the hardships, it is unclear why Daria repudiated the contract or if she has any sort of reason for not wanting performance complete. The question says it was unjustified and so there likely is not. On the other side, Percy has done nothing wrong and appears to have performed adequately. Daria arguably could have to pay more under a restitutionary theory if there is no specific performance (the $20,000 in received benefit as opposed to the initial $15,000 under the contract), so it would not be harder to enforce. However, it may be difficult because of their soured relationship, but that should not be a strong equitable argument considering Daria caused this potential issue.

Feasibility

Lastly, specific performance must be feasible to enforce. Courts consider how long the contract will last, the amount of supervision required, and other related factors. Here, the contract would only take one more month and 100 more hours. This is relatively short for a contract, and the parties could just come back in a month or so to a court to show it was enforced. Daria might argue the court would not want to spend this time, but that could apply to almost any specific performance remedy, and if a 1-month service contract with clear plans/designs already made by Percy is not feasible, then almost any specific performance would not be.

Disposition

While feasibility is not a clear issue, performance would likely be feasible. The biggest issue is whether a court thinks a legal remedy is inadequate. If there is something special about Percy completing this project, then a court will likely order specific performance. If it is just any other landscaping project, it will likely hold that damages (discussed above) will suffice.

QUESTION 1: SELECTED ANSWER B

Applicable Law

It must first be determined what applicable law applies to the contract involved in this dispute between Percy (P) and Daria (D).

Rule: The Uniform Commercial Code applies to contracts for the sale of goods. All other contracts are governed by the common law, such as services contracts and contracts for the sale of land.

The contract between P and D involved the design and installation of landscaping for an exclusive housing development that D owned. As such, this is a contract for services, which makes the common law applicable and governing.

Conclusion: The common law applies.

Contract Formation

A contract is an agreement that is legally enforceable. A valid contract requires an offer, acceptance, and consideration.

The facts state P and D entered into a valid written contract, thus there was a valid contract between them.

Conclusion: There was a valid contract formed between P and D for the design and installation of landscaping.

Anticipatory Repudiation

Did Daria breach the contract by anticipatorily repudiating?

Rule: When one party unequivocally and unambiguously indicates to the other contracting party before the time for performance arrives that they are not going to perform on the contract, this is considered an anticipatory repudiation and a total breach of the contract. The non-breaching party is entitled to all remedies at this time so long as the non-breaching party has not already fully performed their part. If the non-breaching party has in fact fully performed their duties under the contract when the anticipatory repudiation is made, they must then wait until the time for performance to seek remedies.

Two months into the project, Daria "unjustifiably repudiated the contract." This will be regarded as a material and total breach, and at that time P was entitled to all remedies available.

Conclusion: D breached the contract by anticipatorily repudiating, and P is entitled to all remedies at this time.

Remedies

What remedies may P seek from D?

A party may seek legal, restitutionary, and equitable remedies depending on the facts and circumstances of the case.

Legal Remedies

What legal remedies is P entitled to?

Rule: Legal remedies take the form of monetary damages.

Compensatory Damages

Compensatory damages are a common legal remedy in contracts disputes. They can be in the form of expectation damages, consequential damages, and incidental damages, as well as reliance damages.

Expectation damages seek to place the non-breaching party in the position he would have been in had there been no breach. They seek to provide the non-breaching party with his expectations under the contract.

Consequential damages are a form of compensatory damages that are more special in nature and result from the non-breaching party's particular circumstances. These must be known to both parties at the time of contract formation in order for the non-breaching party to be able to recover them.

Reliance damages are used when expectation damages and consequential damages are too speculative and uncertain. They provide the non-breaching party with damages in the amount of how much that party spent in performance and reliance on the contract.

All contract damages must be causal (but for causation), foreseeable at the time of contracting, certain, and unavoidable (non-breaching party's duty to mitigate).

Expectation Damages for the Contract Price

The contract payment price was $15,000. Expectation damages for P would be $15,000 because this is what he expected to receive had the contract been fully performed by both parties.

Consequential Damages for the Photographs

P will also argue that he is owed consequential damages for the loss he incurred due to not being able to photograph the completed gardens and landscaping which he planned to include in his project for an article he planned to propose to Beautiful Yards and Gardens. Since this loss is not a direct expectation damage, P will have to show that the damages are causal, foreseeable, certain, and unavoidable. He will argue that they are causal because D breached the contract only two months into the deal when the work was not yet completely done; he is no longer able to photograph the entire landscaping project and use it in his article which he plans to propose to the magazine. But for the breach, P would be able to have taken the pictures and included them in his article to propose to the magazine. However P will have a hard time arguing that the damages were foreseeable and certain. He may try and argue that these damages were foreseeable to both him and D because he agreed to a reduced fee only because D agreed to let him take the pictures of the completed landscaping project. If P can show that D was aware of the fact that he wanted to use the pictures in a proposal to magazine, he may have an argument this loss was foreseeable to both him and D. Also the fact that he accepted a significantly lower fee might suggest that D was in fact aware that that the photographs were an important "payment" for P. P normally charged $100 per hour for his work and planned to work 100 hours on this project a month for three months. Thus, his normal fee for such a project would have been $30,000, but instead he charged D only $15,000 because she agreed to allow him to photograph the landscaping. He anticipated "that publicity from the article would more than compensate him for his reduced fee." P will argue further that his damages are certain because they amount to $15,000 (the difference between his usual fee of $30,000 for this type of project and what he agreed to with D, $15,000). D will counter that these damages are not certain because they are too speculative. It would be hard to determine and set a monetary amount for how much P would have received in publicity from the article. D can also argue that P only planned to use the pictures in a proposal to propose to the magazine, and that P was not even definitely given an article spot in the magazine.

Regarding the factor of unavoidable, a party is under a duty to mitigate damages. P did in fact mitigate damages by securing a different project with Stuart in the third month that paid him $1, 5000 and took 15 hours to complete. However P will argue that he could have completed this project at the same time as D's, thus is this is in fact the case, then P's damages would not be offset by the $1,500 he earned from the other job because he could have done both projects at the same time, thus he still lost out on the profits from D's breach.

Conclusion: P may have a claim that he is entitled to $15,000 for the loss in being able to photograph the completed project, but there are issues as to the foreseeability and certainty of these damages.

Consequential Damages for the $30,000 Tammy deal

P will also argue that he is owed consequential damages for the $30,000 deal with Tammy. P was negotiating with tammy to landscape her property for $30,000 but once Tammy learned of the unjustifiable repudiation by D she stopped negotiating. P will have to argue that but for D's breach, he would have secured the landscaping job with Tammy for $30,000. The facts do state that "once Tammy learned what happened" she immediately stopped negotiation which suggests that this news caused her to stop negotiating with P. However, P may have some trouble arguing that these damages are foreseeable because D may not have known at all that P was also negotiating with other individuals at the time for similar projects. P will try and make the argument that he is entitled to these damages because D should have known or even did in fact know that by breaching a major landscaping deal for an exclusive housing development news of this would spread and could affect P's reputation in the industry and lead others to refrain from doing business with him under the assumption that he was not an ideal business man since a previous client backed out of a contract with him. This could appear to others to be that P is not skilled and qualified to do landscaping jobs. These damages are likely certain because they were negotiating for an amount of $30,000 for the project and P can also rely on his past business deals to show this amount was accurate. There is no issue as to unavoidability here because there was no way P could have mitigate the loss from the Tammy deal.

Conclusion: P may have a claim for the $30,000 in lost profits from the deal with Tammy, but again these damages likely may be considered too speculative since the parties were only in the negotiations stage.

Incidental Damages

In addition to compensatory and consequential damages a party is always entitled to incidental damages which cover costs directly associated and incidental to the breach. In a contracts case this is usually expenses in negotiating with other parties for completion of the contracted for work.

If P incurred any costs or expenses in finding new work such as with Stuart as well as if he spent any more or time looking for other work to mitigate his losses from D's breach he would be entitled to such damages as well.

Conclusion: If P incurred any damages incidental to D's breach he can recover these in addition to receiving compensatory, expectation, and consequential damages.

Reliance Damages

P has a strong case for expectation damages amounting to $15,000, but he may have some trouble proving lost profits from the photographs and also the deal with Tammy. Instead of recovering such damages, P could elect to recover reliance damages, which would amount to all the costs P incurred thus far in reliance on the contract. Such expenses would include money spent on landscaping tools and items such as bushes and plants and flowers. It seems likely that this amount would be less than the $15,000 and potentially the consequential damages, so P likely would elect to recover those since they would be more money for him.

Conclusion: P could receive reliance damages and incidental damages in lieu of expectation and consequential damages.

Restitutionary Remedies

Restitutionary Remedies can be legal and equitable. Legal restitutionary remedies are applicable here. If a contract is breached or in fact no contract was formed or if a contract later fails for some reason and is no longer enforceable a party can still recover for the value of their services so that the other party will not be unjustly enriched. The value of this is based on the value of the party's services even if this amount is more than they were entitled to under the contract. Restitutionary remedies would be in lieu of legal remedies.

P could also elect to recover restitutionary damages instead of the above legal damages. These would be based on the fact that he completed two months' worth of work on the project at the time of breach. P estimated spending 100 hours of work on the project each month, thus he likely spent 200 hours on the project at the time of breach. P can argue that the value of his services was $100 an hours since this is what he normally charged for his work. As such P would be entitled to $20,000 in restitutionary remedies since D has received the benefits of P's work over the past two months. This would prevent D from being unjustly enriched. The fact that P's hourly rate under the contract was only $50 per hour would not stop P from being able to recover for $100 per hour of work so long as P can demonstrate that the value of his services was $100 an hour, which as discussed above, he likely can do.

Conclusion: P could seek the restitutionary remedy of restitutionary legal damages for $20,000 for the value of his work conferred upon D to prevent unjust enrichment.

Equitable Remedies

Specific Performance

Since P ideally would like to finish the project with D he would most likely argue for the equitable remedy of specific performance. Specific performance is a court order which mandates that a party perform their duties and obligations under the contract. A plaintiff is entitled to specific performance if they can show the following elements:

1. There is a valid and enforceable contract between the parties with terms certain and definite;

2. The non-breaching party has fully performed on the contract, is ready, willing, and able to perform, or their performance has been excused.

3. The legal remedy is in adequate;

4. The remedy is feasible; and

4. There are no defenses to the contract.

Valid, Enforceable Contract with Terms Certain and Definite

P can easily show there was a valid enforceable contract between P and D with terms certain and definite because the parties entered into a "valid written contract." The terms are certain and definite because P was to design and install landscaping for an exclusive housing development for an amount of $15,000 which was to be payable upon completion. He estimated work would take approximately 100 hours a month over the course of three months. All the essential elements such as payment, performance, duration of the contract, and the parties are specified.

Conclusion: P will be able to show there was a valid, enforceable contract with terms certain and definite between the parties.

Fully Performed

P can show he has performed two months' worth of work under the contract, and that he is ready willing and able to finish the project and continue performance if allowed by D. He has also taken other jobs which further indicate his abilities to perform landscaping work and his willingness to do so. Also P has said he ideally would like to finish the project.

Conclusion: P has fully performed.

Inadequate Legal Remedy

An inadequate legal remedy is involved when the sale is for a piece of land since all land is unique or for goods that are unique because they are rare or one of a kind. Also goods may be unique when the circumstances make them so. When the item of the contract is unique then legal damages remedies are inadequate.

P likely will have a hard time arguing that he cannot be compensated by legal damages. Money would be able to make P whole again and compensate him for his losses that resulted from the breach. P may try and argue that he has lost out on a $30,000 contract with Tammy and also much publicity from a proposal and article in magazine and that these damages may be considered too speculative and uncertain as consequential damages for him to prove in court, and thus he cannot be legally compensated by monetary damages for these losses. However, it seems likely this argument would fail.

Conclusion: Legal remedy is likely adequate.

Feasible Remedy

Negative injunctions where a party is prohibited from doing something are easy for a court to enforce. Affirmative mandates are harder to monitor and supervise, thus they pose a problem for the feasibility of ordering specific performance. Also parties are not usually entitled to specific performance when the contract is for personal services.

Here, the contract is for personal services but P seeks to be able to do these services. Usually when the plaintiff seeks for the breaching party to perform services under the contract by specific performance the court will deny this remedy. Because P only has one month left to finish work on the landscaping there is the possibility that the court may make D allow P to finish his project since D only has to pay D.

Conclusion: There may be a feasibility issue.

No Defenses

If there is a defense to the enforcement of a contract, the court will not award specific performance. Such defenses include statute of frauds, statute of limitations as well as equitable defense including unclean hands and laches.

The facts do not implicate any defenses to this contract. The contract was in writing thus there is no statute of frauds issue. Additionally the contract need not be in writing and signed by the party charged since it is not required to be under the Statute of Frauds.

Conclusion: There are likely no defenses to the contract.

Overall Conclusion on Specific Performance: P may be entitled to specific performance, but a court likely would find legal damages to be adequate and also for the remedy to be not feasible, and thus deny this remedy.

Overall Conclusion: As discussed above, P is entitled to the legal remedies of compensatory damages in the form of expectation damages and possibly consequential damages in addition to incidental damages. P could instead elect to recover reliance damages or restitutionary damages.

Question 2

Pete was a passenger on ABC Airlines (ABC), and was severely injured when the plane in which he was flying crashed because of a fuel line blockage.

Pete sued ABC in federal court, claiming that its negligent maintenance of the plane was the cause of the crash.

At trial, Pete's counsel called Wayne, a delivery person, who testified that he was in the hangar when the plane was being prepared for flight, and heard Mac, an ABC mechanic, say to Sal, an ABC supervisor: "Hey, the fuel feed reads low, Boss, and I just cleared some gunk from the line. Shouldn't we do a complete systems check of the fuel line and fuel valves?" Wayne further testified that Sal replied: "Don't worry, a little stuff is normal for this fuel and doesn't cause any problems."

On cross-examination, ABC's counsel asked Wayne: "Isn't it true that when you applied for a job you claimed that you had graduated from college when, in fact, you never went to college?" Wayne answered, "Yes."

ABC then called Chuck, its custodian of records, who identified a portion of the plane's maintenance record detailing the relevant preflight inspection. Chuck testified that all of ABC's maintenance records are stored in his office. After asking Chuck about the function of the maintenance records and their method of preparation, ABC offered into evidence the following excerpt: "Preflight completed; all okay. Fuel line strained and all valves cleaned and verified by Mac." Chuck properly authenticated Sal's signature next to the entry.

Assuming all appropriate objections and motions were timely made, did the court properly:

1. Admit Wayne's testimony about Mac's question to Sal? Discuss.

2. Admit Wayne's testimony about Sal's answer? Discuss.

3. Permit ABC to ask Wayne about college? Discuss.

4. Admit the excerpt from the maintenance record? Discuss.

Answer according to the Federal Rules of Evidence.

QUESTION 2: SELECTED ANSWER A

1) Wayne's Testimony about Mac's question to Sal

Logical Relevance; in order to be logically relevant, the evidence must make a fact that is of consequence in determination of the action more or less probable than without the evidence.

Here the evidence with regard to Wayne's testimony is highly relevant in that it tends to establish that Mac's (M) supervisor Sal (S) had notice of a potential problem with the aircraft prior to flight. Moreover, the second part of the statement shows, the ABC had the opportunity to do a systems check that was part of the routine operation, but ultimately failed to do so. It thus makes it more probable that ABC's employees were negligent in maintaining the aircraft, because S had notice of a problem and took no corrective action.

Legal Relevance - relevant evidence may be excluded if its probative value is substantially outweighed by the danger of unfair prejudice, waste of time, or confusion of the issues. Here ABC will argue that the evidence is highly prejudicial to ABC since it demonstrates that one of its employees noted a problem and stated, that corrective action should be taken. This is unlikely to be well received by the court, since, it is prejudicial, but not unfairly so, since it does not tend to arise the emotions or passions of the jury. Further, the evidence is highly probative in that one of its employees noticed a potential problem and recommended corrective action. As such, the statements about Mac's statements are legally relevant with the probative value not being substantially outweighed by unfair prejudice.

Hearsay: hearsay is defined as an out of court statement offered for the truth of the matter asserted. Here the statement by M was made out of the current proceeding in court, thus it was made out of court. The first part of Mac's statement is an assertion and thus definition be considered a statement. However the second part of the statement with regard to the systems check is actually a question (further explained below), and as such is not an assertion. Accordingly it would fall outside the definition of hearsay as discussed below. Finally, both parts of the statement may be being offered for their truth. That M noticed a problem and cleared out the fuel lines, and that M asked whether they should conduct a full systems check. This would be offered to show that there was actually a problem detected in the aircraft.

Alternatively however, Pete (P) could argue that he is offering this evidence not for its truth, but only for the purpose of showing the effect on the hearer (S). As such, P is only showing that S had notice of a potential problem and failed to take corrective action. If the evidence were offered only for this purpose, it is admissible and not hearsay.

Assuming that P wants to offer the evidence for its truth (that there actually was a problem detected:

a) First part of statement regarding fuel reading and clearing the gunk from the line
Because the first part of the statement is hearsay, it will be inadmissible unless a hearsay exception applies, or the federal rules deem the statement Non-hearsay under an exemption.

Hearsay within Hearsay - when there are multiple levels of hearsay - each independent level of hearsay must be satisfied either by an exception or exemption.

1st Layer - The reading on the fuel gauge. ABC might try to argue that this is an independent level of hearsay, and is an out of court statement being offered for the truth of the matter asserted. This argument would be unavailing however, since gauges which simply provide readout of data (which is not entered by a human) are not considered statements under the traditional hearsay definition. As such the first layer with regard to the fuel indicator would be deemed non-hearsay and would be admissible.

2nd layer - The statement itself

A statement that is made by a party opponent is admissible against that party when introduced by an opposing party. Further, within this exception, an employee's statement related to a matter of employment, while within the scope of employment are exempt from the hearsay definition under this exemption. Similarly, the statements by spokespersons or agents for an individual can be admitted under this exemption. In sum, under the FRE, statements under this exemption are deemed non-hearsay and can be offered for the truth of the matter asserted.

Here the statement made by Mac is was made while he was employed with ABC and related directly to matter of his employment - the mechanical evaluation of the plane before flight. As such it would be deemed non-hearsay and admissible.

Present sense impression - a statement made while contemporaneously perceiving and event and describing that event may be admissible under the present sense impression exception. Here, the statement involves M relaying what he just read and the actions he took on the line. If it was made right after the observations, which it appears to be, it would also be admissible under the present sense impression hearsay exception.

b) Second part of statement with the question regarding the systems check

Here as indicated above, M is actually asking a question, as to whether they should perform a systems check As such it would fall outside the hearsay definition regarding. A statement under the hearsay definition requires an assertion. As such a question cannot be considered hearsay, and would be properly admissible.

In sum, the evidence of Mac's question is properly admissible both for its truth and for the effect on the hearer to show negligence.

2) Wayne's Testimony about Sal's answer

Logical Relevance; in order to be logically relevant, the evidence must make a fact that is of consequence in determination of the action more or less probable than without the evidence.

Here the evidence is clearly logically relevant, it shows that S believed that the gunk wouldn't cause any problems, and more importantly did not take any corrective action upon hearing the findings of Mac.

Legal Relevance - relevant evidence may be excluded if its probative value is substantially outweighed by the danger of unfair prejudice, waste of time, or confusion of the issues. Here, there does not seem to be any danger of unfair prejudice, and thus is legally relevant.

Hearsay - an out of court statement offered for the truth of the matter asserted.
Here the statement is made out of court and is likely being offered for the truth of the matter asserted, namely that as the supervisor, S took no corrective action with regard to the plane.

Because it is hearsay it will be inadmissible unless an exception applies.

Non-hearsay, as statement by part opponent (an employee). As defined above, the statement by S will be deemed a statement of party opponent (ABC) since it related to a matter of employment (inspecting the aircraft) and was made while S was employed with ABC. As such, it will be deemed non-hearsay and is properly admitted.

3) ABC inquiry to Wayne about college

Logical Relevance; in order to be logically relevant, the evidence must make a fact that is of consequence in determination of the action more or less probable than without the evidence. Here the evidence is relevant because it tends to impeach the credibility of

Mac a testifying witness. As such it logically relevant because it may make the jury not believe his testimony, and impact the outcome of the proceeding.

Legal Relevance - relevant evidence may be excluded if its probative value is substantially outweighed by the danger of unfair prejudice, waste of time, or confusion of the issues. Here, the jury may give unfair weight to the evidence, and discredit Wayne's (W)'s testimony. However, it is unlikely a court would find this unfair prejudice, and it probative value is high, since it tends to demonstrate W has been untruthful in the past. As such it would be legally relevant.

Impeachment - prior instances of uncharged conduct - probative of truthfulness - on cross-examination a party is permitted to inquire in specific instances of uncharged prior bad acts if they are probative of truthfulness. It bears noting however, that counsel is bound by the witnesses answer and may not provide extrinsic evidence to prove up the prior bad act.

Here, ABC's counsel is asking W about a specific instance of uncharged conduct - the lying in the course of a job application. Because the lying on a job application with regard to whether W went to college links directly on W's truthfulness as a witness, it is properly admitted. Additionally, since ABC's counsel did not try to introduce extrinsic evidence of the bad act, its form of introduction into evidence was also proper.

4) Excerpt from the maintenance record

Logical Relevance; in order to be logically relevant, the evidence must make a fact that is of consequence in determination of the action more or less probable than without the evidence. Here the evidence is relevant in that it demonstrates that the fuel lines were cleaned and the preflight checks were completed. As such it is relevant, to show that proper care was taken before flight, and less likely ABC was negligent in performing maintenance.

Legal Relevance - relevant evidence may be excluded if its probative value is substantially outweighed by the danger of unfair prejudice, waste of time, or confusion of the issues. Here there are no issues with danger of unfair prejudice; the evidence is also legally relevant.

Hearsay - an out of court statement offered for the truth of the matter asserted. Here the maintenance records are made out of court; they are a statement and are being introduced for the truth of the matter asserted. Specifically, that the maintenance was in fact performed. As such they will be inadmissible unless a hearsay exception or exemption applies.

- Hearsay within hearsay: here there are two levels of hearsay. The first is Mac's entries and the second is the business record itself, each must independently satisfy the hearsay exception.

Statement by Party Opponent

Here the entries by Mac would fall not fall under the statement of party opponent exception because they are being offered by ABC and not P. As such an alternate exception must be used.

Business Record Exception - a report that is created within the regular course of business, is recorded contemporaneously or near after the action of the business, and has indications of reliability can be offered under the business record exception. The business records will be inadmissible if they contain entries by a person who is not under a business duty to report, or are completed with anticipation of litigation.

Here, the custodian of records is proffering the business records. The custodian testified how the records were prepared and their method of preparation. Assuming there were no indicators of untrustworthiness the records are properly admitted. It bears mentioning that the custodian can properly authenticate the signature if he was familiar with the handwriting of Sal. Additionally, the hearsay within hearsay problem is alleviated because the business record exception covers all employees who are creating and contributing to the record who fall under the business duty. As such, M's statements would be properly admitted within the business record.

QUESTION 2: SELECTED ANSWER B

1. Ok to Admit Wayne's testimony about Mac's question to Sal

Relevance = The testimony is logically and legally relevant.

For an evidence to be admissible, it must be relevant. To be relevant, the evidence has to have any tendency to make any fact that is of consequence to the determination of the action more or less probable than without the evidence. Here, Wayne's testimony is most likely logically relevant because Mac's question ("Shouldn't we do a complete systems check of the fuel line and fuel valves?") shows that Mac and Sal, both ABC employees, was on notice that Mac thought they should do a complete systems check of the fuel line and fuel valves. Because Mac has stated that he just cleared some gunk from the line, he probably though more gunk would exist in other parts of the fuel line and valves. If ABC employees thought this way, then this could be relevant to prove that ABC knew that plane had some fuel line blockage problem before operating.

Even if the evidence is relevant, court may not admit the evidence if its probative value is <u>substantially outweighed</u> by unfair prejudice, waste of time, or confusion. Here, ABC would argue that this was only a question by Mac, and it does not indicate whether Mac actually thought there would be Gunk in other parts in the fuel line and valves. ABC would further argue that this question would confuse the jury (if this is a jury trial) to think that the employees actually thought there would be gunk in other places in the fuel lines and valves. However, Wayne's testimony is relevant, and is not substantially outweighed by any unfair prejudice. Although it would prejudice ABC, it is not unfair since opposing party's evidence would most likely be prejudicial to the other party due to nature of the adversarial setting of the trial.

Hearsay = The testimony is either not hearsay or falls under an exception

Hearsay is an out of court statement offered to prove the truth of the matter asserted. Statement can be a conduct or <u>question</u> as long as it is intended by the declarant to communicate something. Here, Mac's question was made outside of the court. Pete would argue that Mac's question is not hearsay because it is a question. However, this question appears to be communicating. Mac stated that he just cleared some gunk from the line, and asked Sal if they should do a complete systems check of the fuel line and valves. Because of his previous statement before the question, Mac's question seems to communicate to Sal that they should be doing some systems check to see if other gunk exists elsewhere. Thus, Pete's argument that this is not hearsay because it is a question will not be too good.

It is not hearsay if the purpose of introducing the statement is not to prove the truth of the matter asserted but to show effect on the listener. Here, this is double-edged sword for Pete. Pete can probably get this in if he argues that this question should be admitted to show the effect on Sal. However, he also wants this question admitted for the truth of the matter asserted to show that Mac most likely thought that gunk existed elsewhere in fuel lines and valves. Thus, Pete can use this argument, but probably is not a good one to make.

The most successful argument would be that this statement falls under a hearsay exemption of statement of party opponent. Statement of party opponent can be admissible even if it is an opinion statement. An employee's statement can be admitted against an employer if the statement was made during the employment and statement describes a matter within the scope of their employment. Here, Mac was employed as an ABC mechanic when he made his question. Also, his statement directly related to his scope of employment as a mechanic because he was talking about doing some system check on the plane. Thus, his question would be admissible as a hearsay exemption of statement against party opponent.

Pete can also use a hearsay exception of present sense impression. A statement describing a condition or event while the declarant is perceiving the condition or event or immediately thereafter is admissible under hearsay exception. Here, Mac stated that he just cleared some gunk from the line, and asking a follow up question to his work. Thus, Pete can argue that Pete was asking that question pursuant to his observation of his clearing of some gunk. ABC would argue that the question pertains to some future work that Mac is thinking about doing, so it does not relate to Mac's present sense impression of his past work completed. Even if ABC has a better argument here, this statement will pass the hearsay hurdle as a statement against party opponent.

Ok to Wayne's testimony about Sal's answer

Relevance = Sal's statement is logically and legally relevant

Here, Sal's statement is logically relevant because it can show negligence of ABC. Sal was notified by Mac that the plane had some gunks, but decided not to do system check because "a little stuff" (i.e., gunks) is normal for this fuel. Pete would argue that ABC knew about the gunks and decided not to clean or do any further systems check. Thus, it bolsters Pete's claim of negligent maintenance of the plane by Mac when he was on notice that the gunk was present in the fuel line. Thus, this is logically relevant.

Additionally, this statement is not substantially outweighed by any unfair prejudice. ABC may argue that little gunks in plane is normal, and this evidence may mislead the jury to think that having little gunk would cause problems.

Although this evidence is prejudicial, this is not unfair because jury can weigh the evidence after it is admitted.

Hearsay = this is not a hearsay statement and falls under a hearsay exception

Here, Sal's statement is a hearsay. His statement was made outside of the court; it was intended to communicate to Mac that little gunk is ok and that it would not cause problems; Pete is introducing this statement for the truth that Sal knew about there being some gunk and little gunk would not cause problems. Pete can argue that he is not offering this statement for the truth of the matter asserted but that Sal knew of some gunks and affirmatively decided not to conduct a system check even after being put on notice. In such a case, this statement would be admitted as non-hearsay.

Like Mac's question, Sal's statement would fall under <u>statement against party</u> <u>opponent.</u> Sal made this statement when he was employed by ABC and it was within the scope of his employment as an ABC supervisor. As a supervisor, he would ordinarily make decisions on whether to do a systems check of the fuel line and valves, and his statements regarding decision not to do such check and reasoning behind such decision would be constituted as statement within his scope of employment. Thus, Sal's statement would be not a hearsay statement.

Pete can also argue that Sal's statement is <u>then-existing state of mind</u> hearsay exception. A statement of past mental or physical condition or then existing statement of mind is admissible even if it is a hearsay statement. Here, Sal is telling Mac to not worry because little gunk will not cause any problems. This shows Sal's lack of worry at the time the statement was made with respect to little gunk in the fuel line system. Thus, Sal's statement would also fall under this hearsay exception.

3. Ok to permit ABC to ask Wayne about college

Relevance

This evidence of Wayne's lying on his job application is relevant because it goes to the credibility of the witness testifying in the court. Here, if Wayne is shown as a liar, it is relevant because then his other testimony cannot be fully trusted. Also, it is not outweighed by unfair prejudice. Jury can determine how much weight to give to a witness who has been impeached.

Leading Question ok here

Leading question is permitted on direct examination in certain circumstances, but is generally allowed in cross-examination. Here, Wayne is being cross-examined, so it is ok for ABC's counsel to use leading questions.

Character Evidence vs. **Impeachment** = Impeachment with prior misconduct related to lying

Character evidence is almost never allowed in civil cases except for few exceptions. Character evidence is given to prove that the person has acted in conformity with his character. However, under right circumstances this is ok if the purpose is to impeach the witness. A witness can be impeached with his prior misconduct related to lying. This impeachment can only be done on cross-examination and cannot be done with an extrinsic evidence. Here, Wayne is on cross-examination, so it was ok for ABC to ask Wayne about his lying on his job application about graduating from college.

4. Ok to admit the excerpt from the maintenance record

Relevance

The maintenance record is relevant because it shows that preflight check was completed with all okays. The record also shows that fuel line strained and all valves were cleaned and verified by Mac. This shows proper maintenance on the part of ABC to counter Pete's negligent maintenance claim. Also, it is not substantially outweighed by any unfair prejudice.

Authentication proper

When non-testimonial evidence is being introduced, it must be authenticated (i.e., prove the evidence is what it purports to be). This can be done several ways. One way is for a custodian of the record to testify to the creation or how the record gets maintained. Here, the maintenance record has been properly authenticated by Chuck, ABC's custodian of records. He testified that all ABCs maintenance records are stored in his office and discussed about the function of the maintenance records and their method of preparation. Also, facts indicate Chuck properly authenticated Sal's signature next to the entry.

Best Evidence Rule

When a written document is introduced as an evidence, courts usually allow the original document or its duplicate (photocopy or another method to re-create the original) to be admissible to prove the content of the written document. However, handwritten copy is not admissible in lieu or an original or a duplicate. Although it is not clear whether the original maintenance record is being introduced, but it would be reasonable to assume that either an original or a duplicate is being introduced.

Hearsay

This maintenance record is hearsay. It is made outside of the court. It was a statement intended to communicate that preflight check was completed, fuel line was strained and all valves were cleaned. ABC is offering this written statement for the truth of matter asserted so that proper maintenance has been conducted. To be admitted, it must fall under a hearsay exception.

ABC would argue that it falls under a hearsay exception of business records. To be a business record exception, it must be (1) a statement of diagnosis, opinion, condition, event, (2) kept at a regularly conducted business activity, (3) made at or near the time matter observed, (4) by personnel who had personal knowledge or gotten the information from someone who had duty to report, and (5) it is regular practice for business to make such record. Here, the maintenance records had statement of plane's condition because the maintenance was completed and the fuel line was strained and all valves were cleaned and verified. Also, it was kept at a regularly conducted business activity because it would be safe to assume that such preflight maintenance records are kept. Although it doesn't say when the record was created, it is reasonable to assume that these records are maintained as Sal and Mac do maintenance checks. Also, Sal as a manager probably has duty to report the maintenance record. Chuck also testified that all ABC's maintenance records are kept in his office, so it would be safe to assume that it is regular practice for ABC to make and keep these types of records. In conclusion, the maintenance records probably fall under business records hearsay exception.

Question 3

Alice's and Bob's law firm, AB Law, is a limited liability partnership. The firm represents Sid, a computer manufacturer. Sid sued Renco, his chip supplier, for illegal price-fixing.

Renco's lawyer asked Alice for a brief extension of time to respond to Sid's interrogatories because he was going on a long-planned vacation. Sid told Alice not to grant the extension because Renco had gouged him on chip prices. She denied the request for an extension. Sid also told Alice that he'd had enough of Renco setting the case's pace, so he wasn't going to appear at his deposition scheduled by Renco for the next week, and that he'd pay his physician to write a note excusing him from appearing. Alice did nothing in response.

In the course of representing Sid, Alice learned that Sid planned a tender offer for the publicly-traded shares of chipmaker, Chipco. Alice bought 10,000 Chipco shares. By buying the 10,000 Chipco shares, she drove up the price that Sid had to pay by $1 million. When Alice sold the 10,000 Chipco shares, she realized a $200,000 profit.

1.   What ethical violations, if any, has Alice committed regarding:

    a. The discovery extension? Discuss.

    b. The physician's note? Discuss.

    c. The Chipco tender offer? Discuss.

    Answer according to California and ABA authorities.

2.   What claims, if any, does Sid have against Alice, AB Law, and Bob? Discuss.

QUESTION 3: SELECTED ANSWER A

Governing Law: California is governed by the California Rules of Professional Responsibility as well as certain sections of the business code. The ABA has promulgated its Model Code of Professional Responsibility as well.

(1) What ethical violations, if any, has Alice committed regarding (1) the discovery extension, (2) the physicians' note, or (3) the Chipco tender offer?

Discovery Extension:

Duty of Fairness: An attorney has a duty of fairness to the opposing party to act in good faith. While an attorney has no duty to accept all requests made by opposing counsel if not required, and while an attorney has a competing duty to her client to act in the client's best interests and should advocate for her client's interests zealously, denial of a good faith request for a short extension may be considered a breach of A's duty of fairness to opposing counsel.

Here, Alice ("A") represents Sid ("S") in suing Renco ("R"). R's attorney has requested a brief extension to respond to interrogatories. The reason for R's request is to go on a long-planned vacation. Without a showing that R's counsel has continuously attempted to delay the litigation by asking for continuances and extensions, A's duty of fairness likely requires her to accept such brief extension. Her denial is based on her client's order that it not be granted for no other reason than "because R had gouged him on chip prices". Because if R's counsel requested an extension from the court based on good reason it might well be granted, it is improper for A to require such unnecessary resort to the court. A has likely violated her ethical duties of fairness.

Duty of Loyalty: An attorney has a duty of loyalty to always act in her clients' best interests and not to engage in conflicts of interest or compete with the client.

Here, A will likely argue that her duty of loyalty to S requires that A not fail to acquiesce to her client's requests. However, the duty of loyalty does not extend this far. An attorney must not advocate for her client to the point that it causes her to make other ethical violations.

Scope of Decision-Making: While the client has the right to state which claims he or she wishes to pursue and make major decisions regarding settlement or whether to plea, etc., it is within the attorney's scope of authority to determine the proper strategy for effectuating these goals.

A should not allow S to "order" her to deny the extension based on no substantive reason. This is within A's scope of authority to decide, and A should not acquiesce to a bad-faith denial of a good-faith request. If A and her client cannot agree on the scope of representation, withdrawal from the case may be appropriate to avoid A being pulled into improper conduct.

Physician's Note:

Duty of Candor/Honesty: An attorney must not make any false representations to the court or opposing counsel, and must not allow her client to make any false representations to the court.

Here, A has stated that he is going to bribe his doctor to get a note to excuse him from appearing at his deposition. This will constitute a fraud upon the court because it is not true that D is unavailable. Further, there is no valid reason for S to fail to appear at his deposition. An attorney can breach his or her ethical duties by failing to speak when she has a duty to counsel her client against illegal or fraudulent activity and advise him that he or she cannot be a part of such conduct. Here, when A failed to respond to S's statement, she impliedly acquiesced in his proposal. This is an ethical violation because it will cause A to participate in a fraud upon the court and will violate her duty of candor.

Withdrawal: An attorney must withdraw from a case when she learns of conduct that will constitute a crime or fraud that will necessarily involve the lawyer's services. If it will not involve the lawyer's services, the attorney may but does not need to withdraw.

Here, paying one's doctor to write a false note excusing him from appearing may constitute such improper behavior that reflects poorly upon the profession. Such conduct is clearly in bad faith and relates directly to the representation, directly involving A. Thus, A should have withdrawn from the representation had she not been able to dissuade S from failing to appear at his deposition for a fraudulent reason because she will necessarily be involved.

Duty of Confidentiality: An attorney has a duty of confidentiality not to disclose any information related to the representation of the client. However, there is an exception to this rule which allows disclosure if the attorney learns that the client plans to commit a crime or fraud. Further, California imposes a duty on an attorney who has learned that his client plans to commit a crime or fraud to attempt to dissuade the client from his proposed actions and further, if that fails, to tell the attorney that the attorney plans to disclose the information to the appropriate authorities.

Here, it is unclear the length S plans to go to in order to get him a "note". However, this likely does not constitute an actual crime or fraud, so A likely has no right to breach her duty of confidentiality to her client. Since she has not, she has not violated this rule.

Duty to Diligently Pursue Completion of the Case: An attorney has a duty to diligently pursue a case to completion without allowing it to languish in the court system.

Here, by impliedly acquiescing in S's statement that he plans to fail to appear at his deposition, this will require a further scheduling out of a deposition at a time convenient for the parties and court reporter. This is a bad faith delay of the case that constitutes breach of A's ethical duties.

Chipco Tender Offer:

Duty of Loyalty: As stated above, an attorney has a duty of loyalty to her client to always act in the best interests of the client. This includes not acquiring an interest adverse to the interest of the client. California allows an attorney to obtain an interest adverse to that of her client in certain circumstances.

Here, when A learned of S's plan to make a tender offer for the publicly traded shares of Chipco, she immediately purchased Chipco shares and then sold them for a $200,000 profit. A's acquisition of these funds constitutes a breach of A's duty not to obtain an interest adverse to her client's, because the price S had to pay on the shares was raised by one million dollars. A has caused serious financial injury to S by acquiring an adverse interest and essentially taken a profit that should have gone to S. In doing so, A has breached her ethical duties.

Conflict of Interest: An attorney has a concurrent conflict of interest when there is a substantial likelihood that her ability to represent her client will be materially limited by her own personal interests, her duties to another client, a former client, or a third party. An attorney may take on the representation despite the concurrent conflict of interest if the attorney can believes that she can competently and adequately represent the interests of the parties, and if she obtains written consent from all involved parties. California has no "reasonable lawyer" standard and does not require written consent, only written notice, when the interest is personal to the lawyer.

Here, in gaining a personal interest in Chipco, A may have created a conflict that will materially limit her representation of S. However, A may argue that this is a deal on the side and is unrelated to the subject of the litigation in which she represents S; and further, A may argue that ownership of the shares has no bearing on her representation of S. If the court determines that she has acquired a conflict of interest, A has breached her duty by failing to get written consent. In California, she has further breached her duty by failing to give written notice to S.

Duty of Confidentiality: See above. In using confidential information S provided to her in telling her about the tender offer for her own benefit, A may have breached her duty.

(2) What claims, if any, does S have against A, AB Law, and B?

Limited Liability Partnership: A limited liability partnership is a special type of partnership that affords limited liability to all its partners, created by filing a Statement of Qualification with the Secretary of State. In a limited liability partnership, the individual partners are not personally liable for any damages sustained by the partnership itself.

A: See above.

A will be personally liable for her own torts.

B: See above.

Because B is a partner in an LLP, he has limited liability. Thus, S will have no claim against Bob ("B") A's partner.

AB Law:

Authority: A partnership is liable for its partner's actions if the partners have authority to act for the partnership. Authority may be actual (express or implied), apparent, or ratified. Actual authority exists where a reasonable person in the agent's position would believe he had the right to act on behalf of the business. This may be express, through an agreement, or implied, through actions or conduct. Apparent authority exists where a reasonable person in the shoes of the third party believed that the person had authority to act. Ratification occurs where no authority exists but the business has adopted the contract through action such as accepting its benefits. A partner in a partnership has both apparent and implied authority to act on behalf of the partnership.

Here, as a partner of AB law, A has actual authority to act on behalf of the partnership. Her acts taken in the scope of her law practice will thus subject the partnership to liability. Thus, A will both be personally liable for her own torts, and S will further be able to collect against AB Law for her actions.

Unjust Enrichment:

Here, S will sue A personally and AB Law for likely malpractice for losses caused by her breaches of her duties. Her misconduct has led to a loss by S of 1 million dollars, and has resulted in a gain to A of $200,000. In equity, a court may under unjust enrichment theory disgorge profits made by someone and impose a constructive trust. A constructive trust is not truly a trust but is an equitable remedy imposed by the court which forces the wrongdoer to hold unjustly realized profits in trust for the benefit of the rightful owner. Because she has been unjustly enriched by action taken in breach if her duties to S, the court will likely impose a constructive trust on the profit realized by A and will thus force A as trustee of these funds to distribute them to their proper owner, S.

Intentional Interference with a Business Expectancy: Intentional interference with business expectancy occurs where a person knows of a business expectancy of another party and knowingly interferes with that expectancy, resulting in damages. Here, S had planned a tender offer with C. Her actions in purchasing Chipco shares may constitute an interference with this expectancy with S, although A will argue that this expectancy is not yet an enforceable contract and that she has a valid defense of fair competition. This will be balanced by the court.

QUESTION 3: SELECTED ANSWER B

Discovery Extension

Scope of Representation

A client usually determines the ends (goals) of a representation, whereas the lawyer generally determines the means (legal strategies). If a client is insisting upon actions that the lawyer does not wish to take, the lawyer may limit the scope of employment through informed written consent by the client. Here, it appears that Alice let Sid influence her legal decision-making by telling her to deny the request for an extension to respond to Sid's interrogatories. This type of decision should normally be decided by the lawyer because it falls into legal strategy. Although it is permissible for the lawyer to seek the client's input, the final decision should ultimately be left up to the lawyer. Alice let Sid control the litigation means.

Fairness to Opposing Counsel/Adverse Parties

A lawyer should treat opposing counsel and adverse parties fairly during the representation. A lawyer should not engage in certain actions if it is known to be for the purpose of harassing or making a task unduly burdensome for opposing counsel/adverse party. Here, Sid told Alice to reject the request to extend the time for answering the interrogatories. Renco's lawyer asked for a reasonable "brief extension" to respond since he was going on a long-planned vacation. This seems to be a reasonable request and is not an attempt by Renco's attorney to delay for an improper purpose. Sid's reasons for wanting to deny the extension, however, would be considered improper. He denied the request because Renco had "gouged hi on chip prices," so he was acting out of spite. He told this directly to Alice, so she knew his improper motives. She should have counseled him to allow the extension since it was a reasonable request and made clear that Sid's motives were improper. Because she did not do this, Alice violated her duty of fairness to Renco and its lawyer by furthering her client's improper purpose.

That being said, a lawyer does owe a duty to her client to diligently dispose of the case (work productively and not delay unnecessarily). If for some reason the extension requested was unreasonable, or it had been one of many requests for extensions, then perhaps Alice would be justified in denying the request. She has a duty to her client to make sure that his case is handled efficiently and effectively. The facts do not suggest this was the case, but if it was, then again it is possible she may not be in violation of an ethical duty.

Physician's Note

Duty of Candor

A lawyer owes a duty of candor to opposing counsel, adverse parties, and the court. A lawyer must not submit evidence that she knows to be false or make a false statement of fact or law that she knows to be untrue. If she makes such a statement without knowing it is false and later learns of its true nature, the lawyer has a duty to correct the evidence or testimony.

Sid told Alice he was not going to appear at his deposition for Renco the next week because he'd had enough of Renco setting the case's pace. He also told Alice that he was going to pay his physician to write a note excusing him from appearing at the deposition. Alice did nothing in response. Alice knows that Sid is not sick and that he just does not want to attend the deposition. He is going to get a fake doctor's note written to excuse him, so this would be false "evidence" or a false statement of fact being presented to the opposing side. Alice has a duty not to allow such false information to be presented to the other side. That being said, there is a conflict with her duty of confidentiality to Sid not to disclose his statements to her since they were made during and related to the representation.

A lawyer owes a duty of confidentiality to her client for anything related to the representation, even if not made by the client. Under the ABA, a lawyer may reveal confidences if the client persists in engaging in criminal or fraudulent conduct that will result in death or serious bodily harm, or if the lawyer's services are being used to perpetuate a crime or fraud by client that will result in serious financial harm. California does not have an exception for financial losses. Neither of these exceptions appears to be present. Sid's actions will not cause harm to anyone to the extent of death or serious bodily harm. It may pose a financial burden on Renco because they have to pay the lawyer for time that was spent preparing and now it will be postponed, but the amount spent is not likely to satisfy the requirement of financial harm under the ABA. Therefore, since no exception applies, Alice cannot reveal Sid's confidences.

So Alice cannot reveal the confidences but she must not present false evidence. What she should have done is counseled Sid by trying to get him to show up for the deposition and not pay a doctor to make a false note. If that did not work, then she should have withdrawn from the representation since he was persisting in engaging in fraudulent conduct. If the withdrawal would be harmful to Sid, a court might not let her withdraw and it may request why she is choosing to withdraw. If that is the case, then Alice may reveal Sid's confidences regarding the letter. Because Alice did not take these steps and said nothing when Sid mentioned a fake doctor's note, she breached her duty of candor to Renco and its lawyer.

Duty of Fairness

Again, as mentioned earlier, Sid has improper motives for wanting to submit the doctor's note and not attend the deposition. He wants to regain control of the pace of the litigation and is acting out of spite toward Renco for the price he was charged for the chips. Alice should know based on the comments Sid has made to her that he only wants to delay the case for improper purposes. Because she is aware of this, Alice is violating her duty of fairness to opposing counsel and adverse party.

Chipco Tender Offer

Duty of Loyalty

A lawyer owes a duty of loyalty to her client. If the interests of another client, the lawyer, or a third party materially limit the lawyer's ability to effectively represent the client, then she has a conflict of interest. The lawyer must act in the best interest of the client. Tied with the duty of confidentiality mentioned below, a lawyer also cannot use information learned during the course of the representation to the disadvantage of her client.

Alice used the information she learned from Sid during the representation that Sid was going to make a tender offer to her advantage by purchasing shares of the stock and driving up the price. Alice benefitted by realizing a $200,000 profit while Sid had to pay $1 million more than he would have before she purchased the shares. Alice was looking out for her interests first and negatively impacted her client's interests in the process. Because she subordinated her client's interests to her own, Alice violated the duty of loyalty she owed to Sid.

Duty of Confidentiality
A lawyer owes a duty of confidentiality to her client. She must not reveal any information related to the representation that she learns, and she must not use that information to the disadvantage of her client.

Here, Alice learned while representing Sid that Sid planned to tender offer for the publicly-traded shares of Chipco. She used this information to Sid's disadvantage by purchasing 10,000 Chipco shares, which drove up the price that Sid had to pay. Although this purchase is unrelated to the representation, it involved information learned during the representation. The duty of confidentiality is broad and covers any information related to the representation. Alice may try to argue that this information is unrelated to Sid's illegal price-fixing claim against Renco, but it would likely be found to be covered by the duty of confidentiality. Price-fixing involves the market of that particular industry, and if Sid intends to make a tender offer for a competitor chipmaking company, it would affect the same market involved in the litigation that she is representing Sid for against Renco. Therefore, a court would find that the information is attenuated but still within the realm of the confidences covered by the duty of confidentiality. Since Alice used the information against Sid to his disadvantage, she violated her duty of confidentiality.

Sid v. Alice, AB Law, and Bob

AB Law is a limited liability partnership (LLP). A limited liability partnership operates almost exactly the same as a general partnership except the partners in an LLP are not personally liable for the debts of the partnership like they are in a general partnership. Therefore, the partnership is liable for the negligent acts (but not intentional torts) of its partners but the other partners are not personally liable for different partner's negligent acts or debts of the partnership. A partner always remains liable for her own actions.

Alice

Alice obviously violated several of her ethical duties. The breach of the duty of loyalty that she committed against Sid by purchasing Chipco stock caused actual pecuniary harm to her client. This was an intentional act on Alice's part. Under her breach of the duty of loyalty, since she financially benefitted from her actions, realizing a $200,000 profit from buying and selling her shares of stock, she would be liable to Sid for profits realized as a result of her breach of the duty of loyalty. Therefore, Alice is personally liable for $200,000. She may also be liable for the harm caused to Sid by the breach. Sid had to pay $1 million more than he otherwise would have if Alice had not purchased the shares. But for Alice's purchase of the stock, Sid would not have had to pay $1 million more for the tender offer. It was also foreseeable to Alice that if she purchased the shares, it would drive the price of the stock up for Sid's tender offer. Therefore, she is also liable as the actual and proximate cause of Sid's loss due to her breach. Alice is personally liable for $1,200,000 to Sid.

As for a specific claim, Sid may be able to claim misappropriate. Alice was in a relationship of trust and confidence with him as a fiduciary. Sid had nonpublic information that most people would find material, meaning it was affect whether someone would purchase a stock or not. Sid did not tell this information to Alice for an improper purpose and surely did not anticipate she would use the information to purchase stock. Therefore, Sid would not be a tipper and Alice cannot be a tippee. But she can be a misappropriator since she was in this fiduciary relationship with the source of the non-public material information and she purchased stock in reliance on that information. Therefore, she is liable to Sid for the same amount of damages mentioned above because they were profits that would need to be disgorged and harm caused from her misappropriation.

Bob

Because these actions were taken by Alice, even if the partnership is liable, Bob cannot be personally liable for the harm caused by Alice. It is a limited liability partnership, so partners are not personally liable for the debts of the partnership or torts of other partners. Therefore, Sid does not have any claims against Bob.

AB Law

A partner is an agent of the partnership and thus can bind the partnership to certain obligations. The partnership is also liable for the negligence or non-intentional torts committed by partners while in the scope of employment for the partnership.

Here, Alice was working as Sid's lawyer when she learned the information that she misappropriated from him. Her actions, however, would likely be considered beyond the scope of her employment as a partner. She took the information and used it for personal reasons. If she had, for example, not filed an important document on time resulting in a dismissal with prejudice, then Sid could sue for malpractice and the LLP would be liable because the claim arose from her duties as a lawyer. This harm caused to Sid was not because of Alice's actions as an attorney for Sid. Therefore, a court would likely find that the LLP is not liable for Alice's actions and Sid has no claim against AB Law. If the court did find her actions were within the scope of her duties as a partner, then AB Law would also be liable for the losses Sid incurred.

Question 4

One summer afternoon, Officer Prowl saw Dan, wearing a fully buttoned-up heavy winter coat, running down the street. Officer Prowl ordered Dan to stop. Dan complied. As Officer Prowl began to pat down Dan's outer clothing, a car radio fell out from underneath. Officer Prowl arrested Dan and took him to the police station.

At the police station, Officer Query met with Dan and began asking him questions about the radio. Dan stated that he did not want to talk. Officer Query responded that, if Dan chose to remain silent, he could not tell the District Attorney that Dan was cooperative. Dan immediately confessed that he stole the radio.

Dan was charged with larceny. He retained Calvin as his attorney. He told Calvin that he was going to testify falsely at trial that the radio had been given to him as a gift. Calvin informed Dan that he would make sure he never testified.

Calvin filed motions for the following orders: (1) suppressing the radio as evidence; (2) suppressing Dan's confession to Officer Query under *Miranda* for any use at trial; and (3) prohibiting Dan from testifying at trial.

At a hearing on the motions a week before trial, Dan, in response to Calvin's motion for an order prohibiting him from testifying, stated: "I want to represent myself."

1.   How should the court rule on each of Calvin's motions? Discuss.

2.   How should the court rule on Dan's request to represent himself? Discuss.

QUESTION 4: SELECTED ANSWER A

1. Ruling on Calvin's Motions

Motion to Suppress the Radio as Evidence

Fourth Amendment Protections

The Fourth Amendment, incorporated to the states through the Fourteenth Amendment, protects individuals against unreasonable searches and seizures of their person, home, and personal effects. A seizure occurs when an individual's freedom of movement is limited by an officer such that the person would not feel free to leave the officer's presence. A search occurs when an officer gathers information in which the individual has a reasonable expectation of privacy, such as a physical search of the person's body, a search of the person's home, or eavesdropping on private conversations through wiretapping. However, if the officer is in a location in which he is entitled to be, he may observe the person's conduct or identify contraband that is within plain view, since people do not have a reasonable expectation of privacy for things they disclose to the public, such as speaking on a public street. The general standard for reasonableness to affect a search or seizure is probable cause, although lesser standards apply in certain circumstances, as discussed below. The Fourth Amendment generally requires that police officers obtain a search warrant before searching a person and an arrest warrant before an arrest to ensure that the probable cause standard is met.

Terry Stop

Under the Supreme Court decision in Terry, an officer may stop and search an individual based on less than probable cause. A "Terry stop" is a reasonable search under the Fourth Amendment when two conditions are satisfied. First, the officer must have reasonable suspicion, based on specific and articulable facts, that the individual is engaged in criminal activity in order to stop the person. The officer may then question the individual. In order to search the person, the officer must have reasonable suspicion, based on specific and articulable facts, that the person is armed. This is reasonable because if the person is armed, the officer is in possible danger.

Seizure

A seizure occurs when an officer restricts the freedom of movement of a suspect such that the individual would not be free to leave the officer's presence. The court will take into account all of the circumstances, including the officer's language and tone and the setting in which the confrontation took place. However, merely being in a physically confined area (such as a bus) will not make the officer's interaction with a person into a seizure. If the officer orders the individual to stop, the seizure does not occur until the person complies with the officer's instructions and his movement is actually restrained.

Here, Officer Prowl ordered Dan to stop while he was running down the street. He did not approach Dan and ask him to voluntarily speak with him. Rather, ordering "stop" would be interpreted by a reasonable person to be a use of police authority to restrain Dan's movement such that Dan could be subject to penalty if he refused. Dan complied with Prowl's order and actually stopped. Thus, a seizure occurred.

Reasonable Suspicion to Stop

The seizure of Dan will be reasonable under the Fourth Amendment, per Terry, if Prowl had reasonable suspicion to stop Dan. In order to satisfy the Fourth Amendment, Officer Prowl must have reasonable suspicion that Dan is engaged in criminal activity. This must be more than a mere hunch or an anonymous tip that the officer has no reason to trust. The officer must be able to identify specific facts that demonstrate objectively the reasonable suspicion to stop the person.

Here, Dan was running down the street wearing a fully buttoned-up heavy winter coat on a summer afternoon. It is objectively unusual to see someone wearing such a coat during the summer, and Prowl's experience would likely indicate to him that people use such coats to conceal contraband, such as stolen property or drugs. Further, Dan was running. Because of the coat, it would seem unlikely that Dan was running for exercise, since he would be overly hot during the summer.

Because these facts, taken together, indicate that Dan was acting objectively suspiciously, Prowl had reasonable suspicion to stop Dan.

Search

A search occurs when an officer infringes upon an individual's reasonable expectation of privacy. The individual's person is always an area in which the person has a reasonable expectation of privacy unless that expectation has been reduced for some reason, such as in prisoners and parolees. We do not have any indication that Dan was a parolee or on probation. Thus, when Officer Prowl patted Dan down, a search occurred.

Reasonable Suspicion to Perform Pat-Down

Under Terry, Prowl's search of Dan will be reasonable if he had reasonable articulable suspicion that Dan was armed. Although Dan's activity was objectively suspicious, he did not do anything and we have no indication that Prowl had prior knowledge that would make it objectively likely that Dan was actually armed. Prowl did not even speak with Dan after ordering him to stop, but immediately began a pat-down. Prowl would argue that Dan's bulky coat could easily have concealed a weapon, and Prowl's search was thus for self-protection. However, a physical search based on no independent facts suggesting that the person is armed is only reasonable following an arrest. Here, Dan was not arrested when Prowl performed the search.

Prowl's search of Dan was not based on reasonable articulable suspicion and was therefore a violation of Dan's Fourth Amendment rights.

Exclusion of Evidence

Evidence seized in violation of an individual's Fourth Amendment rights will generally be excluded in any subsequent criminal prosecution of that individual. The exclusionary rule operates as a deterrence mechanism to discourage police officers from committing constitutional violations. Although there are some circumstances in which the Supreme Court has concluded that the deterrent effect of the exclusionary rule is too inadequate to justify exclusion (such as knock-and-announce violations), the exclusionary rule operates in the Terry stop circumstances. Any contraband that was discovered as a result of an illegal search subject to the exclusionary rule will be excluded from evidence.

Here, Prowl violated Dan's Fourth Amendment rights when he unreasonably searched Dan. Therefore, the court should order that the radio be suppressed.

Motion to Suppress Dan's Confession

Fourth Amendment

First, Dan would argue that the Fourth Amendment violation directly led to his confession, and thus the confession should be excluded under the "fruit of the poisonous tree" doctrine discussed above. However, the Fourth Amendment exclusionary rule operates to exclude physical evidence rather than statements. Thus, Dan's confession would not be excluded by the Fourth Amendment.

Fifth Amendment Protections

The Fifth Amendment right against self-incrimination protects suspects from being compelled to make statements against their own penal interests. The Supreme Court in Miranda interpreted this protection to require the police to effect certain warnings to individuals who are subject to custodial interrogation at the hands of police to offset the inherently compelling pressures of police interrogation.

Miranda Warnings

Police officers must give each suspect warnings about his rights once he is subject to custodial interrogation. The warnings must inform the suspect of his right to remain silent, his right to an attorney, and that the attorney will be provided for him if he cannot afford to pay.

Custodial

The "custodial" element is satisfied if the person is subject to police custody at the time of questioning. Once the individual is arrested, he is generally understood to be in police custody. Even before an arrest, the suspect may be subject to custody if he is being restrained in a formal setting, such as a police station, and is not told that he is free to leave at any time. The suspect need not have been indicted or charged for the custody element to be satisfied.

Here, Dan had been arrested and taken to the police station, where Query began questioning him. Because Dan was in a formal setting and had actually been arrested, the custodial element is satisfied.

Interrogation

The "interrogation" element requires that the police actually be asking the defendant questions that would be reasonably likely to lead to an incriminating response. A question such as whether the suspect would like a drink of water or whether he was comfortable would not constitute interrogation.

Here, once Dan was in custody, Query began asking him questions specifically about the radio. Thus, Dan was being interrogated.

Because both elements of Miranda are satisfied here, Query violated Dan's Fifth Amendment right against self-incrimination by failing to read him Miranda warnings.

Dan's Statement That He Did Not Want to Talk

Once an officer has read the suspect his Miranda rights, any express invocation of those rights must be strictly honored by the officers, who must then stop interrogating the suspect.

Here, Query should have read Dan his rights. Dan's explicit statement that he "did not want to talk" likely qualifies as an invocation of his right to remain silent. Because Query continued to interrogate Dan following Dan's express invocation of his right to remain silent, Query violated Dan's Fifth Amendment rights.

Exclusion of Statement under Fifth Amendment

The remedy for a Fifth Amendment violation is an exclusion of the improperly obtained confession. However, generally speaking, any physical fruits of the confession, such as evidence seized in reliance on statements made in the confession (such as the location of contraband) are not excluded. Further, the statement may still be used to impeach the suspect if he were to testify in the criminal case.

Here, Dan confessed that he stole the radio. Because Dan's Fifth Amendment rights were violated, the statement should be excluded from the prosecution's case-in-chief, although it may still be used to impeach Dan.

Voluntariness

The Fifth and Fourteenth Amendments of the Constitution also protect individuals against compulsory statements. A statement is compulsory if it was made involuntarily. An involuntary statement could be made as a result of legal compulsion (such as a subpoena to testify before a grand jury) or by improper police tactics, such as physical violence, threats, or promises that the suspect will not be prosecuted if he confesses. Although Calvin did not move to suppress the statement on voluntariness grounds, Dan would be wise to do so, since exclusion on voluntariness grounds would prevent the statement from being used against Dan on cross-examination.

Here, Query told Dan that he "could not tell the District Attorney that Dan was cooperative" if he refused to speak. Although this statement does not explicitly promise Dan that he would not be prosecuted based on the statement, Dan would argue that Query suggested that he could guarantee different penal consequences based on whether Dan confessed. Query would say that he merely suggested a statement he could make to the prosecution, not that the prosecution would react in any specific way.

Because Query did not make any actual promise that Dan's penal outcome would be different, the statement was likely voluntarily made.

Exclusion of Statement for Voluntariness

If Dan's statement were involuntarily made, the statement itself would be excluded for all purposes, including impeachment. Further, any physical fruits of the statement would be excluded as well. Thus, because Dan wants to testify at trial, he should still argue that the statement was involuntary, even if this argument is likely to fail.

Motion to Prohibit Dan from Testifying

Defendant's Right to Testify

Each defendant has a constitutional right to testify in his own trial. Although an attorney has a professional ethical obligation to counsel his client not to lie on the stand, the lawyer cannot prevent the client from doing so. Under the ABA authorities, the attorney must seek to withdraw from the representation if he knows that the client intends to perjure himself. The court could then grant leave to withdraw, but may also decide that efficiency and justice require continued representation.

Thus, the court should rule against Calvin's motion to prevent Dan from testifying. However, it would be proper under the ABA rules for Calvin to seek to withdraw from representing Dan.

2. Dan's Request to Represent Himself

Sixth Amendment Protections

The Sixth Amendment right to counsel protects a criminal defendant's right to be represented by an attorney in all critical stages of prosecutory action by the state. The Sixth Amendment right includes the right to counsel of choice or to decline the right of representation if the defendant is competent to refuse.

Right of Self-Representation

The Sixth Amendment includes a right of self-representation. The court must grant the right if the defendant is competent.

Competence to Stand Trial

The general rule is that if the defendant is competent to stand trial, he will be found competent to represent himself. To be competent to stand trial, the defendant must understand the nature of the proceedings against him and be aware of the consequences of the proceedings.

Here, we have no facts suggesting that Dan has a mental defect that would affect his competence. Thus, the competency to stand trial is satisfied.

Competence for Self-Representation

The Supreme Court has stated that competence for the purpose of self-representation does not require the defendant to be legally sophisticated or be able to do an objectively good job representing himself. Although the Court has recognized that most defendants would be better served by counsel than by self-representation, the Sixth Amendment guarantee requires the court to allow the defendant to represent himself, regardless of whether the court finds that his action is in his own best interest.

Thus, although Dan does not appear to have any particular legal knowledge or skills, such knowledge is not required to trigger the constitutional right to self-representation. Therefore, the court must allow Dan to represent himself.

Advisory Counsel

The court may require that the individual be assigned advisory counsel to assist him. The role of advisory counsel is to provide the defendant with legal advice and information, but advisory counsel is not allowed to make the strategic decisions that appointed or retained counsel may, such as choosing to call only certain witnesses (other than the defendant) or present certain evidence. The advisory counsel role serves as a layer of protection for a self-representing defendant in order to protect the integrity and efficiency of the judicial process.

Thus, although the court must allow Dan to represent himself, it could choose to appoint Calvin or another attorney as Dan's advisory counsel.

QUESTION 4: SELECTED ANSWER B

1. HOW SHOULD THE COURT RULE ON EACH OF CALVIN'S MOTIONS

(1) Suppressing the Radio as Evidence

Exclusionary Rule

Where evidence is obtained unlawfully under the Fourth, Fifth, or Sixth Amendments, that evidence is generally inadmissible against the accused. In Mapp v. Ohio, the Supreme Court held that the exclusionary rule is incorporated against the states. Moreover, under the fruit of the poisonous tree doctrine, all evidence obtained as a result of an invalid search or confession is also suppressed unless the government can prove (i) an independent basis; (ii) inevitable discovery; or (iii) an intervening act of free will.

Fourth Amendment Search and Seizure

The Fourth Amendment provides that a person be free from unreasonable searches and seizure of their persons, homes, papers, or effects. To that end, Dan (D) should be able to successfully argue that he was unlawfully seized and that the radio must be excluded as the fruit of an invalid seizure.

(1) State Action

The Fourth Amendment is only triggered by state action. Thus, a state or federal police officer or a private officer that has been deputized by the city or state must be the actor in order to render the Amendment applicable. Here, Officer Prowl (OP) appears to be a state police officer and hence the state action requirement is satisfied.

(2) Search / Seizure

A "seizure" occurs under the Fourth Amendment where the circumstances of the encounter are such that a reasonable person would not feel free to decline the encounter. A "search" under the Fourth Amendment only occurs where the D has a reasonable expectation of privacy in the area and thing searched, or where there is a government intrusion into a constitutionally protected area.

Seizure. Here, D was ordered to stop by OP. A police officer may ask a person if they are willing to talk, at which point the person is free to decline and is not seized. However, where an officer commands a person to stop, their authority as a police officer is such that a reasonable person does not feel free to decline the encounter. Thus, D was seized by OP when he was commanded to stop and he did, in fact, stop.

Search. Here, D does not have a reasonable expectation of privacy in his movement on the streets. OP is free to follow him as much as he wants. However, D does have a reasonable expectation of privacy in the things he keeps out of public view, hidden under his coat. Merely stepping out onto the street does not render everything in D's possession "public." In this case, OP also intruded upon a constitutionally protected area, i.e., D's person. By patting down the outer clothing that D was wearing, OP intruded on his person and searched him under the Fourth Amendment.

Thus, if there is not a valid basis under the Constitution for this search and seizure, the evidence was obtained in violation of the Fourth Amendment and must be suppressed.

(3) Warrant Requirement

A search or seizure is generally unreasonable unless the police have a warrant, or an exception to the warrant requirement applies. A warrant must be founded on (i) probable cause; (ii) state with particularity the persons and places to be searched; and (iii) be executed in a valid manner. Where a warrant that is otherwise invalid is relied upon in good faith by the arresting officers, the search or seizure will be upheld as long as the warrant was not: (i) so lacking in probable cause or particularity as to render reliance unreasonable; (ii) obtained by fraud on the magistrate; or (iii) the magistrate was impartial.

Here, there was no warrant to arrest or search D. Thus, the search and seizure are unconstitutional unless an exception to the warrant requirement applies.

(4) Warrant Exceptions

Terry Stop. An officer may engage in what is known as a temporary "investigative detention" under the Supreme Court's Terry framework, provided the officer has reasonable suspicion of criminality on the part of the D which is based on "articulable facts."

Here, the only facts that are given is that D was running down the street one summer afternoon wearing a fully buttoned, heavy winter coat. The fact that it was summer and D was wearing a fully buttoned up winter coat is certainly suspicious. Indeed, a reasonable person would almost have to assume that the purpose of wearing such a coat would be to hide evidence of contraband. If it is warm outside, as it usually is in the summer, a coat would be unnecessary. On the other hand, D may live somewhere like San Francisco where summers can be quite cold; D may have had a cold or some condition that makes him cold; or D may have been training for a sporting event such as wrestling where people force themselves to sweat more. The Court has held that headlong flight from an officer after seeing the officer is evidence sufficient to help support reasonable suspicion, but merely running has never been held to be reasonable suspicion absent additional facts.

Nevertheless, given that D was running down the street and wearing a coat that was fully buttoned during the winter, a court would likely find that the officer had reasonable suspicion--but certainty not probable cause--to detain D for a short period of time to investigate the potential criminality.

Terry Search. An officer that has reasonable suspicion of criminality based on articulable facts may also conduct a Terry search of the D, provided he has reasonable grounds for believing that the D is armed and dangerous. A Terry search must be limited to a pat-down of the outer clothing of the D, and must be limited to a search for weapons. In order to remove evidence that is not a weapon, the officer must have probable cause to believe the other evidence, e.g., drugs or a car stereo, is illegal.

Here, there is no real evidence that D is armed and dangerous. He was running wearing a coat, which--as discussed above--is sufficient to find reasonable suspicion that D just committed some type of theft offense and is trying to conceal the contraband in his coat. However, D will argue there is really no reason to believe that he was armed at this point. OP cannot simply claim he thinks D is armed because he seemed sketchy. On the other hand, OP might be able to convince a court that many theft offenses are committed with a weapon and hence that D could reasonably have been carrying a weapon. The fact that D was not actually carrying a weapon will not undermine this argument. While this is a close call, a court would likely permit OP to conduct a Terry search here.

The scope of the search seems permissible in this case, as OP merely patted down D's outer clothing. As he did so, a car radio fell out. The car radio is not a weapon, but may be admissible under the plain view doctrine, discussed below. In any event, the search and seizure itself was not unconstitutional.

Plain View. The Plain View doctrine applies where (i) the police have a right to be where they are viewing; and (ii) they see evidence and it is immediately apparent the evidence is contraband. Here, as discussed above, OP had the right to stop D under Terry, and hence he had a right to be where he was viewing the radio as it fell from D's coat. Moreover, it was immediately apparent to OP that the car radio was contraband. Indeed, D was running down the street, in a coat, in the summer, with a car radio hidden inside his coat. The radio was quite apparently stolen and hence admissible under the plain view doctrine.

Consent. While D has a constitutional right not to be searched or seized, the right is subject to waiver, i.e., the search or seizure is not unreasonable if D consents to the search or seizure. Consent must be knowing and voluntary. However, it is not required that one know they have the right to decline the encounter.

Here, D is not likely to be deemed to have consented to either the seizure or the search by OP. Indeed, as discussed above, he was seized. A defendant is not deemed to consent when seized. Moreover, with respect to consent to search, OP just started patting down D's outer clothing. Consenting to questioning is not within the scope of consenting to search. Thus, even if D were deemed to consent to questioning he would not be deemed to consent to the search. In any event, the search and seizure are valid under Terry.

Conclusion
The evidence of the radio is admissible given that the search and seizure were valid under a Terry stop and frisk and the radio fell out of D's coat and was in plain view.

(2) Suppressing Dan's Confession to Officer Query

The Fifth Amendment protects a person from being compelled to be a witness against his or her self. Due to the inherent risks of coercion in police custodial interrogations, the Supreme Court has held that a defendant must be given Miranda warnings before any confessions by the defendant are admissible against the defendant, unless used to impeach.

Miranda Warnings
Miranda is triggered where the D is: (i) in custody; and (ii) interrogated.

Custody. For purposes of Miranda, custody is defined as a place where a reasonable person would not feel free to leave. Moreover, custody is assessed by looking to whether the situation involves the same inherently coercive pressures as stationhouse questioning.

Here, D was arrested and taken to a police station where he was then met by Officer Query (OQ). D had no ability to leave, and no reasonable person would feel free to leave in this situation. Moreover, this is stationhouse questioning, so the inherent pressures that Miranda is meant to protect against are at their pinnacle here. Thus, D is in custody.

Interrogation. Interrogation is defined as any line of questioning that a reasonable officer would find likely to illicit an incriminating response. Here, OQ was asking D questions about the radio. This is clearly questioning that is likely to generate an incriminating response. Thus, D was interrogated.

As both elements of Miranda are met, D was required to receive Miranda warnings. OQ ought to have told him he had the right to remain silent; that anything he said could be used against him in court; that he had the right to an attorney; and that he had the right to have an attorney appointed if he could not afford one. Since D was not warned, his confession is inadmissible against him (unless it is used to impeach him).

Invoking Miranda

D was not warned, but in this case it even seems that he attempted to invoke his Miranda rights. To invoke the right to remain silent, the D must clearly and unequivocally indicate his intent to invoke. Here, D stated to OQ that he "did not want to talk." That may not use the word "remain silent" but no reasonable officer could think that "not want[ing] to talk" means anything other than remain silent. After having said that, OQ tried to coerce him into talking. This is not permitted. OQ must honor D's request and stop talking. By badgering him after he invoked, any later confession is in violation of Miranda. In this case, since D was not even Mirandized, his is irrelevant. However, even if D were Mirandized, the fact that OQ failed to honor his request to remain silent is a separate basis for excluding this statement.

Conclusion

The confession must be suppressed (except for purposes of impeachment). Thus, the court should grant the motion in part, subject to use for impeachment.

(3) Prohibiting Dan From Testifying At Trial

Constitutional Right to Testify in Defense

All defendants have a constitutional right to testify in their defense at a criminal trial. This right trumps any ethical obligation that Calvin (C) has to the court or the profession. Indeed, neither C nor the court can prohibit D from testifying in this situation.

[NOTE: The proper response by C would have been to inform D that he cannot testify falsely and persuade him to testify truthfully. If that failed, C should have tried to withdraw from the representation. If the court failed to allow him to do so, under the ABA C should have then informed the tribunal and allowed the tribunal to take the necessary steps. Under the California rules, no disclosure is permitted. Instead, C should have let D testify and questioned him up until the point he knew he was going to testify falsely, then, at that point, allow D to testify in the narrative and in no way rely upon D's narrative in closing. Under any ethical rule and the Constitution, the prohibition on D testifying is not permitted.]

Conclusion

The court should rule that D be permitted to testify, as a criminal defendant has a constitutional right to testify. The tribunal may take necessary steps to remedy the false testimony, such as requiring narrative testimony.

2. HOW SHOULD THE COURT RULE ON DAN'S MOTION TO REPRESENT HIMSELF

Faretta Motion

The right of a criminal defendant to be represented by counsel was held to require the right of self-representation in Faretta. Where a Faretta motion is timely made, and the court is satisfied that the defendant is competent enough to represent himself, the court is required to respect the dignity of the defendant and allow him to have the right to choose for himself and represent himself. A court may also appoint back-up counsel to assist (but not actually control) the representation, but that is not constitutionally required.

Competence. The Supreme Court recently held that a defendant may be competent to stand trial but nevertheless incompetent to represent himself.

In this case, we have very little information on whether D is capable of representing himself. It appears he was found competent to stand trial, or at least that no such hearing has been conducted to this point. Thus, given no facts indicating that D cannot represent himself, he would likely be deemed competent to stand trial. The judge would have to verify that D was able to understand the charges and the legal issues, but--again--there is nothing in the facts indicating D cannot handle this. The court would also look to the issues between D and C and use this as a further justification for allowing D to represent himself.

Timeliness. A court need not allow a defendant to represent himself if doing so would cause an undue delay in the case. The request must be timely.

Here, D made the request to represent himself after an attorney was appointed and various pretrial motions were made. Indeed, the motion came just a week before trial. To allow D to testify would likely require giving D extra time to prepare the case himself, which would mean that the trial would have to be pushed back. That would interfere with availability of witnesses and with the efficiency of the court and the ability for the prosecution to put on its case. D might also win sympathy from the fact C is not permitting him to put on his case. However, that is more of a reason to substitute counsel than to let D represent himself. In this situation, D would need to show he was immediately prepared to go to trial. Delay of any sort would be sufficient to permit the court to deny his Faretta motion.

Conclusion

Although D is likely competent to represent himself, but the court is likely to deny the motion as untimely, given that the trial date is set for only one week from the date of the motion and given that D would likely need a good amount of time to fully prepare himself for trial.

Question 5

Henry and Wynn married in 2000. During the first ten years of their marriage, Henry and Wynn lived in a non-community property state. Henry worked on writing a novel. Wynn worked as a history professor. Wynn kept all her earnings in a separate account.

Eventually, Henry gave up on the novel, and he and Wynn moved to California. Wynn then set up an irrevocable trust with the $100,000 she had saved from her earnings during the marriage. She named Sis as trustee and Henry as co-trustee. She directed that one-half the trust income was to be paid to her for life, and that the other one-half was to be paid to Charity, to be spent only for disaster relief, and that, at her death, all remaining assets were to go to Charity.

Wynn invested all assets in XYZ stock, which paid substantial dividends, but decreased in value by 10%. Charity spent all the income it received from the trust for administrative expenses, not disaster relief.

Later, Sis sold all the XYZ stock and invested the proceeds in a new house, in which she lived rent-free. The house increased in value by 20%.

Henry has sued Sis for breach of trust, and has sued Charity for return of the income it spent on administrative costs.

1. What is the likely result of Henry's suit against Sis? Discuss.

2. What is the likely result of Henry's suit against Charity? Discuss.

3. What rights, if any, does Henry have in the trust assets? Discuss. Answer according to California law.

QUESTION 5: SELECTED ANSWER A

1. Henry v. Sis

As discussed in #3, Henry does not currently have a personal interest in the trust assets. However, he is the co-trustee of the trust, and this may be sufficient to give him standing as trustee to bring an action against Sis for breach of her fiduciary duty as trustee.

Trust creation

To be valid, an express private trust must have a settlor, an ascertainable beneficiary, res, a valid purpose, and a trustee. However, the court will appoint a trustee if one is not provided for, or the elected trustee declines to serve. Here, Wynn is the settlor, and she has designated herself and Charity as lifetime beneficiaries, and Charity as the remainder beneficiary. Any natural person, entity or government can be a beneficiary of an express private trust. Both are ascertainable beneficiaries because they are either persons or entities expressly named in the trust instrument. The res can be any property or present interest. Here it is the $100,000 from Wynn's separate account. The trust appears to have two purposes: to provide lifetime income to Wynn; and to contribute to disaster relief via Charity. To be valid, a trust purpose must be able to be determined from the trust document, and must not be illegal. Neither of the purposes are illegal and are clear from the trust document. Wynn has designated Sis as trustee and Henry as co-trustee, and from the facts it does not appear that either declined to serve. They must be competent but there is no indication of incompetency in the facts.

Charitable trusts differ in that they must have a charitable purpose: something that contributes to societal good, such as abating hunger, education generally, religion, or the like. The beneficiaries of the trust must be indefinite, not a specific person. Here, because Wynn is a specific person, this could not be a charitable trust.

A valid express private trust was created.

Trustee powers

A trustee has the powers expressly granted in the trust document itself, and those implied in order to effect the purpose of the trust. Here, the trust instrument directed Sis to pay one-half of the income to Wynn, and the other half to Charity. This expressly gave her the power to make these distributions.

Trustee duties

A trustee has the duty of loyalty, to act for the benefit of the beneficiaries solely, and not in her own self-interest or that of third parties. This duty requires the trustee to be impartial as to multiple beneficiaries. Here, Sis has a duty to treat Wynn and Charity impartially. If this were a revocable trust, she would have a primary duty during Wynn's lifetime to Wynn as the settlor, but the trust is irrevocable.

As part of the duty of loyalty, a trustee has a duty not to self deal. Sis is living in the house owned by the trust, rent-free. Thus she is reaping personal benefit from her position as trustee. She has violated her duty of loyalty.

The trustee has a duty of care as well, which requires her to act as a prudent person would in handling their own affairs. This includes the duty to account regularly to the beneficiaries, and not commingle trust assets with her own.

As part of the duty of care, a trustee has a duty to invest the trust res as a reasonably prudent investor would. Under the traditional view, this limited the holdings of the trust to things such as blue chip stock, 1st trust deeds on real estate, government bonds and other conservative and safe investments. Each separate investment was considered separately in determining this. Modernly, the investments are looked at as a whole, and factors such as the need for income, tax consequences, and particular trust purposes are considered. Thus, the court will need to look at how Sis invested the trust res in light of whether the trust was intended more for lifetime income sources, or as a gift to

Charity at Wynn's death, at how the income would affect taxes, at what was reasonable as an investment in light of what was available to invest, at what reasonable investors were doing at the time.

Wynn originally invested the trust assets in XYZ stock, which provided substantial dividend income but lost value overall. This would seem to indicate a preference for lifetime income over growth of the principal.

Henry will need to be able to show that a reasonably prudent investor would not have sold the XYZ stock and invested it in a house. The sale of the stock itself may have been prudent given the loss in value. However, a trustee also has a duty to diversify in order to reduce the risk of loss and enhance income/growth opportunity, as would a reasonable investor. While the duty to diversify may have called for Sis to sell some or all of the XYZ stock, that same duty would generally preclude sinking all of the proceeds into one property. The trust res is then subject to any decline in real estate in the market, and will not benefit from any gains in other potential investments. Sis has probably violated her duty of prudent investment, and has certainly violated her duty to diversify.

The duty to make the res productive requires that Sis put the assets to work for the benefit of the beneficiaries. When she lived in the house rent-free, she violated this duty. The rental income from the house is to be distributed to Wynn and Charity, not retained for her benefit.

Sis has a duty to effect the purpose of the trust, by ensuring that income is maximized, based on the express and apparent intent of the settlor. She has not done so by selling the income stock and buying a house that currently provides no income to the trust.

Because Henry is currently subject to these same duties as co-trustee, he is obligated to prevent the wrongdoing of the other trustee. Thus he has standing to bring an action against Sis for her violations of duty, as a trustee of the trust.

Remedies available

The remedies available against a trustee who has violated their duties includes removal, surcharge for lost income/profits, disgorgement of any benefit wrongfully taken by the trustee. This benefit does not run to Henry, who is acting solely for the trust beneficiaries' benefit.

Henry will seek an accounting for the rent that should have been paid by Sis while living in the house owned by the trust. These funds must be paid personally by Sis. Additionally, he will seek surcharge for the lost income from the XYZ stock or similar investment that would have maximized lifetime income. Sis will have to make up the shortfall in income from her own funds.

Finally, Henry will seek removal of Sis as trustee. The court may then allow Henry to act as sole trustee or may appoint someone else.

Given Sis's breach of duty, the apparent purpose of the trust, the court will allow all of these remedies.

2. Charitable trusts are enforced by the attorney general, rather than by private action. If Charity is a charitable trust, Henry will not have standing to bring an action.

Assuming Henry has standing as the co-trustee of Wynn's trust, he can seek a constructive trust by tracing the funds from the trust to Charity as used for admin purposes. This will mean that Charity's sole duty as trustee of the constructive trust is to use the funds as directed.

3. California is a community property (CP) state. All property acquired during marriage while domiciled in CA or another CP state is presumed to be CP. All property acquired prior to marriage, or after separation, is presumed to be separate property. Additionally, all property acquired at any time by gift, descent, devise or bequest is presumed to be CP.

All property acquired during marriage while domiciled in a non-CP state that would be CP if domiciled in CA, is presumed to be quasi-CP (QCP). At termination of the marriage, to determine the character of property, a court will look at the source of the funds used to acquire property, any applicable presumptions, and any actions by the spouses that may change the character of the assets. A mere change in form does not alter the character of the asset.

Source:

Here, the source of the funds for the house, which is the sole trust asset, can be traced back to the XYZ stock and further, back to Wynn's earnings as a history professor. Because all earnings by community labor are CP, these earnings would be CP if the spouses had been domiciled in CA at the time they were earned. Thus, by definition, they are QCP (defined supra). During marriage, QCP remains the SP of the owning spouse. At divorce or death of a spouse, the character as QCP affects the property determination.

Presumptions:

All assets acquired during marriage are presumed to be CP. However, as noted, the source of the house is earnings that are Wynn's SP until termination of the marriage. Spouses can also take title in ways that raise a presumption, such as a gift to the community, which arises on death of a spouse under Lucas. However, Wynn kept the funds in a separate account, and then created an irrevocable trust with the funds, so no alteration in the title is shown in the facts.

Actions of the spouses

Spouses can by transmutation or other actions alter the character of their own SP. Henry may argue that the change from Wynn's separate account to a trust is such a transmutation. However, a transmutation, to be valid, must be in writing, signed by the adversely affected spouse and clearly express the intent to transmute. This is not evident here, so no transmutation has taken place.

Distribution of assets

At divorce, QCP is treated as CP, and this would entitle Henry to half of the QCP. Death also impacts the character, depending on which spouse dies. If the SP owner (Wynn) predeceases the non-owning spouse, the non-owning spouse may choose their forced share (take against the will) in order to get to QCP assets. However if the non-owning spouse dies first, they have no right to devise the QCP that belongs to the other spouse.

As a result, Henry has no immediate right in the trust assets. In the event of divorce or death of Wynn, he would acquire such rights as are discussed above.

QUESTION 5: SELECTED ANSWER B

1. What is the likely result of Henry's suit against Sis

A trustee owes fiduciary duties of loyalty and care to the beneficiaries of a trust. A trustee may bring suit against a co-trustee for breaching the fiduciary duties, and move to have the violating trustee removed from their position.

A. Duty of Care

Generally, a trustee owes a duty of care to the beneficiaries to act as a reasonably prudent person under similar circumstances. This includes the duty to prudently invest trust property in a manner that will create the greatest return for the benefit of the trust.

i. Prudent investment

A trustee has a duty to prudently invest trust funds so as to increase the benefits from investments for the trust beneficiaries. Here, Sis sold all of the XYZ stock in the trust and used the proceeds to pay for a house. Sis will argue that this is a prudent investment because XYZ stock had decreased in value by 10%, whereas the value of the house has appreciated 20%. This increased the value of the trust property. However, Henry will likely argue that to tie up all of the trust assets in one piece of property which potentially can fluctuate wildly in the real estate market is not a prudent investment. Instead he will argue that Sis should have diversified to different stock from other companies other than XYZ in order to keep a more stable and broad base for the trust property.

Based on these arguments, it is likely that Henry will prevail against Sis in arguing that exchanging all of the stock into one parcel of real property is not a prudent investment.

ii. Duty to diversify

A trustee also has a duty to diversify the stock held by the trust. Here, as discussed above, the trust initially only held XYZ stock. Henry will argue that Sis had a duty to diversify the stock to include stocks from other corporations, and that consolidating the trust assets into one piece of property which is less liquid and potentially subject to market fluctuations in price and value violated the duty to diversify.

A. Duty of loyalty

A trustee is a fiduciary and owes a duty of loyalty to the beneficiaries and the trustor of the trust. Therefore, Sis has a fiduciary duty of loyalty to act solely in the best interest for the trust.

i. Duty to avoid self-dealing

A trustee has a duty to avoid self-dealing with respect to trust assets. The trustee must obtain court approval before the sale of any property which benefits the trustee personally. Here, Sis sold all of the trust assets and used the proceeds from the sale to purchase a house in which she lives in rent-free. She is therefore using trust assets for her own personal benefit, which is impermissible absent court authorization. She has a duty to pay fair market rent to the trust for use of the property in order to avoid a claim of self-dealing.

Therefore Sis has arguably violated her duty to avoid self-dealing

ii. Fairness to all beneficiaries

A trustee also has a duty to act impartially and fairly towards both the income and the principal beneficiaries. The trustee cannot favor one beneficiary over another in terms of their investments or distributions. Here, whereas Wynn and Charity are both income beneficiaries of the trust currently, Charity is the only principal beneficiary after Wynn's death.

(a) "Income"

Income beneficiaries are entitled to cash dividends from stocks, and rents from property held by the trust. Initially XYZ stock issued substantial dividends which are considered income to the trust and distributed to the income beneficiaries. Therefore Wynn and Charity were sharing the substantial income beneficiary. However, as noted above, the stock declined in value and therefore was worth 10% less, therefore reducing the future value for the principal beneficiary.

However, upon changing the stocks for the house, the principal beneficiary would obtain a 20% increase in value of the property. However, Sis is not paying any rent for the property, and therefore Wynn is no longer getting an income from the trust as a result of this change. This change, coupled with the lack of rental payments by Sis, means that Henry will likely be successful in arguing that Sis has violated her duty to act fairly and impartially towards both income and principal beneficiaries.

D. Conclusion

Because of the aforementioned breaches in duty, it is likely that Henry will prevail against Sis in claiming a breach of trust. The trust would likely be entitled to a constructive trust for the unpaid rent that was due on the propety, and Henry may have Sis removed as trustee for breaching her duties of care and loyalty.

2. What is the likely result of Henry's suit against Charity for return of the income

A. Purpose of a charitable gift

A trust must have a valid purpose in order to be properly formed. Here, part of the trust's express purpose at the time of formation was for income from the trust to be delivered to Charity but only go towards disaster relief. Charitiable contributions and trusts are considered valid purposes and therefore the trust is permissible.

B. Violation of a condition by a beneficiary

However, a violation by a beneficiary of an express condition of the trust violates the trust purpose. The court will look at the totality of the circumstances to determine whether the language was intended to merely express a wish on the party of the trustor, or rather if it is an express condition for receipt and use of funds. Here, the trust had an express condition that the share of income given from the trust to Charity was only to be used for disaster relief. However, the beneficiary here instead used the funds for administrative expenses, not disaster relief. The Charity will likely argue that it was only a general wish because they would receive the full benefit of the property upon Wynn's death and therefore should be able to use and dispose of trust income in any manner that benefits the charity. However, Henry will likley argue that the express terms of the trust are explicit in requiring that the funds only be spent on disaster relief. Therefore the beneficiary has violated an express term of the trust.

C. Remedy for violation by a beneficiary

If a beneficiary violates an express term of a trust, the trustee can sue for return of the income used in violation of the trust terms. Therefore Henry would likely prevail in a suit against Charity for return of the income.

3. What rights does Henry have in the trust assets?

All property acquired during marriage in CA is presumed community property (CP). However, property acquired by (1) gift or inheritance; (2) expenditure of separate property funds, (3) the rents, profits, or income derived from separate property; or (4) acquired before the marriage are presumed to be separate property (SP) of the acquiring spouse.

A. Quasi-Community Property

If a married couple acquires property in a non-community property state that would have been community property had the couple been residents of a community property state, such items are considered "quasi-community property" (QCP) and are potentially subject to community property laws if the couple later moves to a community property state. During the marriage, the QCP is treated as SP of the acquiring spouse. However, upon divorce or death of the acquiring spouse, the QCP will be treated as CP and divided equally between the spouses. Upon the death of the non-acquiring spouse, the property will remain the SP of the acquiring spouse.

B. Wages earned during marriage

Wages, earnings, and pensions earned during marriage are considered CP, absent an agreement between the spouses agreeing otherwise. Here, Wynn earned a salary working as a history professor while living out of CA. Regardless of whether she kept the earnings in a separate account, in CA the earnings would be considered CP. The facts do not show that Wynn and Henry had any agreements changing the character of the property. Therefore upon moving to CA, Wynn's earnings are presumed to be QCP. However, as noted above, they retain their SP characterization until death or divorce.

C. The trust assets

Wynn and Henry are still married at the time that Wynn sets up the trust fund with $100,000 of her earnings. Even though these funds are earmarked as potential QCP, during the marriage they are still considered the SP of the spouse who earned them. Therefore at this time, Henry does not have any interest in the trust assets because of the ongoing marriage. Henry will not have any possible rights to the trust assets until death or divorce.

Question 6

Owner owned and operated a small diner where Cook and Waiter worked. After closing one day, Cook called in sick for the following day. Owner knew that an acquaintance, Caterer, owned and operated a catering business. Owner asked Caterer to fill in for Cook. Owner told Caterer: "I want you to run the kitchen for one day. I will pay you your standard catering fee. I just need somebody who knows what he's doing." Caterer agreed, telling Owner, "I'll bring my own knife set, but I assume the kitchen is fully equipped."

Owner did not check Caterer's references. If he had, he would have learned that Caterer's business had once been shut down by the health department.

Caterer went to Owner's diner and started to cook. Patron, a customer, ordered chicken wings from Waiter. Waiter gave the order to Caterer.

A notice posted on the kitchen wall, entitled "Health and Safety Code Section 300 Notification," stated: "To avoid food poisoning, all poultry products must be cooked at a minimum temperature of 350 degrees." Upon observing that the oven was set at 250 degrees, Waiter informed Caterer that the oven should be set at 350 degrees. Caterer responded: "Just worry about waiting tables, and leave the cooking to me." Caterer did not raise the temperature of the oven, and removed the chicken wings shortly thereafter.

Waiter served Patron the chicken wings. Patron ate the chicken wings and suffered food poisoning as a result.

Under what theory or theories, if any, might Patron bring an action for negligence against Caterer, Waiter, and/or Owner, and what is the likely outcome? Discuss.

QUESTION 6: SELECTED ANSWER A

In a negligence case, the plaintiff must show duty, breach, causation, and harm. When the defendant's conduct creates an unreasonable risk of harm to others, a duty of due care is owed to all foreseeable plaintiffs; the defendant must act as a reasonable person to protect foreseeable plaintiffs. Under the majority Cardozo view this duty is owed to all foreseeable plaintiffs, while under the minority view it is owed to all plaintiffs. When the defendant's conduct falls below the relevant standard of care, the defendant has breached his duty. To show cause, the plaintiff must show actual cause (that the plaintiff's injury would not have happened but for the defendant's conduct) and proximate or legal cause (that the plaintiff's injury was foreseeable in that it was a result of the increased risk created by the defendant's conduct/within the normal incidents of the defendant's conduct). Finally the plaintiff must prove that they suffered damages. Here, Patron will be able to satisfy this final requirement of harm/damages with respect to all possible defendants because Patron suffered food poisoning as a result of eating the chicken wings.

Patron v. Caterer

Patron can bring a negligence claim against Caterer for negligently serving Patron undercooked chicken wings. First, Patron could establish the first element of a negligence claim by arguing because Caterer was cooking food to serve to customers at a diner, he owed a duty to all customers who would be eating at the diner to exercise due care/act as a reasonably prudent person in the preparation of their food. Because Patron was a customer at the diner, Caterer thus owed a duty of care to Patron. Caterer breached this duty in multiple ways. First, Caterer failed to exercise due care by not reading and heeding the notice on the kitchen wall that to avoid food poisoning, all poultry products must be cooked at a minimum of 350 degrees. This notice was easy to understand and seems to have been conspicuously posted, and thus a reasonable cook in the kitchen would have read and followed the warning. Second, Caterer was unreasonable in ignoring Waiter's warning that the oven was only set at 250 degrees.

As a cook by profession, Caterer should have known the necessary temperature to cook food at to avoid food poisoning, and even if he didn't there was a notice in the kitchen stating what temperature poultry must be cooked at. Furthermore, as a cook Caterer should exercise due care in making sure that the oven is set at the proper temperature, and even if he were for some reason excused for not noticing that the oven was at the wrong temperature, the fact that Waiter explicitly warned Caterer that the oven was at 250 degrees would negate any possible excuse. Thus, Caterer breached the duty of due care he owed to Patron by cooking the chicken wings in an oven which he knew was only set at 250 and when he knew that the Health and Safety Code required poultry to be cooked at a minimum of 350 degrees.

Moreover, the fact that a Health and Safety Code mandated a minimum temperature of 350 degrees gives Patron another theory on which to show duty and breach. In this case of a violation of a regulation such as this Health and Safety Code, a plaintiff can take advantage of the statutory presumption of negligence. If a plaintiff can prove a defendant violated a statute, that the plaintiff was within the class meant to be protected by the statute, and that the harm caused to plaintiff was of the harm meant to be prevented by the statute, then the duty and breach elements of a negligence case will be presumed. In this case, Caterer clearly violated the statute by cooking the chicken at 250 degrees. The statute explicitly states that it is meant to avoid food poisoning, so the harm caused to plaintiff was indeed the harm meant to be prevented by the statute. Finally, the statute is a Health and Safety Code that is posted in restaurant kitchens, indicating that restaurant patrons are the class of people meant to be protected by the statute. Thus, all the elements are satisfied and Patron can use Caterer's breach of this statute to show duty and breach.

Actual causation is easily established because if Patron had not eaten the chicken wings, she would not have gotten sick ("but for" consuming the chicken wings, she would not have suffered harm). Proximate cause is also straightforward in this case; it is very foreseeable that serving someone chicken wings that have been undercooked will cause that person food poisoning, especially if the person cooking the chicken wings is a professional caterer. Finally, as stated in the introductory paragraph, Patron can easily establish damages because she got food poisoning. Thus, Patron is likely to prevail on a negligence claim against Caterer.

Patron v. Waiter

Patron can also bring a negligence claim against Waiter under the theory that he negligently served her undercooked chicken wings or negligently failed to warn her of the possibility that the wings were undercooked.

Patron would argue that as a waiter, Waiter has a duty to his customers to not serve them food that he knows has a substantial likelihood of causing food poisoning, whether or not he himself is responsible for cooking the food. Alternatively, Patron could argue that Waiter had a duty to warn his customers if he was serving them food which he had reason to believe could cause food poisoning. Waiter would counter that because he was not responsible for cooking the food, he did not have a duty to Patron. However, while it is true that Waiter probably didn't have a duty to make sure that the food was cooked property because it was not his job to cook the food, as a professional waiter he did at least have a duty to either not serve food he had reason to believe would cause food poisoning, or to warn Patron that the food might cause food poisoning. This is because a restaurant patron reasonably relies on their waiter to serve them food that the waiter believes to be safe for consumption. If Waiter had no reason to believe that the chicken would cause food poisoning, he would not have breached his duty to act as a reasonable person with respect to his customers. However, here Waiter knew that the oven was only set at 250 and that the cook had ignored his warning to adjust the temperature. Under these circumstances, a reasonable person exercising due care would not have served the chicken wings, at least not without warning their customer. Thus, Waiter breached his duty to Patron by serving her chicken wings when he knew that they were not cooked at the required temperature.

Patron would argue that actual cause is established because if waiter hadn't served her the chicken wings, she would not have eaten them and gotten sick. Waiter would try to argue that if he hadn't served the chicken wings, a different waiter working that day would have brought them to the table, and he is therefore not a "but-for" cause of Patron's injury. However, the most likely interpretation of this situation is that because Waiter knew that the chicken was undercooked, his duty was not simply to refrain from bringing the chicken to the table but rather to make sure that Patron was not served the chicken or was warned about the chicken; because he was employed as a waiter at the restaurant where Patron was eating and knew of the danger, he cannot avoid liability on that argument. Patron would thus be able to establish actual cause: but-for Waiter's failure to prevent Patron from being served or failure to warn her, Patron would not have eaten the wings and gotten sick. Patron would also be able to establish proximate cause: Waiter knew the oven was only set to 250 degrees and that Caterer had ignored Waiter's warning. It was thus foreseeable that the chicken would be undercooked, foreseeable that if Waiter served the chicken to Patron, Patron would eat the chicken, and foreseeable that if Patron ate the chicken she would get sick. Thus, Patron could establish proximate cause. Damages could be established as above.

Therefore, Plaintiff would also likely win in a negligence action against Waiter for negligently serving her chicken wings that he knew were likely to cause food poisoning.

Patron v. Owner

Patron could bring a suit against Owner either for vicarious liability for Caterer's negligence, vicarious liability for Waiter's negligence, or direct negligence for negligently hiring caterer.

An employer is vicariously liable for the negligence of its employees in the course of their duties. An employer will not be liable for negligence of their employees outside of the duties, nor will someone generally be liable for the negligence of an independent contractor (rather than of an employee). However, someone will still be liable for the negligence of a contractor if the negligence involves a non-delegable duty or an ultrahazardous activity.

Thus, the first question is whether Caterer is an employee or an independent contractor. A court will address this issue by analyzing the degree of care and control Owner exercised over Caterer, taking into account factors such as the length of employment, the nature of the duties, the amount of responsibility retained by and amount of discretion exercised by the employee/contractor, and the nature of payment. In this case, the fact that Caterer was only filling in for Owner for one day while Cook called in sick, was asked only to "run the kitchen for one day," brought his own knives, was paid a one time payment of his standard catering fee, independently owns and operates his own catering business, and does not appear to have been supervised in his duties all support a finding that Caterer was an independent contractor. The fact that aside from the knives Caterer relied on Owner's "fully stocked" kitchen supports an argument that Caterer was an employee; so does the nature of the job, as generally a cook in a restaurant is an employee of the restaurant; however, these facts are not sufficient to support a finding that Caterer was an employee. Thus, Caterer would be found to be an independent contractor.

Therefore, if Patron were to pursue a claim that Owner was vicariously liable for Caterer's negligence, Patron would have to argue that Caterer was performing a non-delegable or inherently dangerous/ultrahazardous function. The latter exception does not apply because while cooking food at a restaurant does have some inherent risks regarding kitchen safety and food poisoning issues, these are not sufficient for a finding that it is ultrahazardous. However, Patron has a chance of prevailing on the argument that the duty of ensuring that food cooked and served to restaurant patrons is cooked to health and safety code specifications is a non-delegable duty. Common carriers and store/restaurant owners are held to have a particularly high duty of care to their customers, and as such some duties are non-delegable. One example of a non-delegable duty is the maintenance of taxicabs: even though taxi drivers and mechanics are independent contractors, the taxi company may not escape liability for negligence in the maintenance of their fleet of cars by claiming that they are not liable for negligence of independent contractors on public policy grounds. Another example of a non-delegable duty, and one that is more relevant to this case, is the maintenance of a store to keep it safe for customers. In that case, if for example a store owner hires an independent contractor to repair a dangerous condition in the store that creates a hazard to customers, the store owner can still be found vicariously liable for the independent contractor's negligence under the theory that maintaining the safety of the premises is non-delegable for public policy reasons. By analogy, the owner of a restaurant could still be found liable for the negligence of an independent contractor regarding ensuring that food is cooked according to health and safety code requirements, because restaurant owners owe a particularly high duty of care to their customers and therefore such duty is non-delegable on public policy grounds.

Therefore, Patron has a good chance of prevailing on the argument that Owner is vicariously liable for Caterer's negligence on the grounds that the duty of ensuring that food served at Owner's restaurant is cooked according to health code specifications is non-delegable. Of course, for Owner to be vicariously liable, it must also be established that Caterer himself was negligent. As discussed above, Patron has a strong case that Caterer was indeed negligent; therefore, this will not be a bar to arguing that Owner was vicariously liable.

Next Patron could argue Owner is vicariously liable for Waiter's negligence. Here there are no facts indicating that Waiter is an independent contractor. Owner might try to argue that the fact that waiters generally earn most of their wages in tips supports a finding that Waiter is an independent contractor and not an employee. However, this is not very persuasive and court would probably find Waiter to be an employee. Thus, if Patron did prevail on her claim against Waiter for negligence, she could also prevail on a claim against Owner for vicarious liability; however, if Waiter were found not to be negligent, Patron would have no such claim against Owner.

Finally, Patron could argue that Owner was directly negligent in hiring Caterer because he did not check Caterer's references. First Patron would have to establish duty. Patron could successfully argue that Owner had a duty to his customers to exercise due care in selecting his employees and independent contractors. Patron could also successfully argue that Owner breached that duty by not checking Caterer's references. A reasonable restaurant owner would check the references of a Caterer before hiring him. Owner would argue that here he was only hiring Caterer for one day, that Caterer owned and operated his own catering business which was evidence that he was a competent caterer, and that Caterer was an acquaintance of Owner so perhaps he had independent, circumstantial knowledge of his competence. However, these arguments are not persuasive; it would not have taken long to check Caterer's references, and given the nature of the work he was being hired to do, it was still reasonably prudent to check his references even though he was only being hired for one day.

Patron would argue that Owner's breach of duty in failing to check Caterer's references was the actual cause of her harm because the facts state that if Owner had checked Caterer's references, he would have learned that Caterer's business had once been shut down by the health department. To prove actual cause, however, Patron would still have to argue that had Owner found this out he would have then chosen not to hire Caterer or would have chosen to supervise Caterer more carefully. The court will likely permit this inference in Patron's favor, and she will thus be able to establish actual cause.

Patron would argue that Owner's breach was also the proximate cause of her harm because it was foreseeable that by hiring Caterer without checking his references, Owner was taking the risk that Caterer was incompetent and could cause harm as a result of his incompetence. Patron would probably succeed on this element. It is established practice in the service industry to check references before hiring. Thus, it is foreseeable that a failure to check someone's references could lead to the type of situation at issue. Finally, damages would be established as above. Thus, Patron is likely to prevail on a direct negligence claim against Owner.

QUESTION 6: SELECTED ANSWER B

In all negligence actions, the plaintiff must establish a prima facie case for negligence, which generally is composed of four elements:

(i) defendant owes a duty to plaintiff,

(ii) that duty is breached,

(iii) the breach is the actual and proximate cause of the injury, and

(iv) damages to the person or property.

All four elements must be established to succeed on a negligence claim.

The duty owed to the plaintiff is a general duty to all foreseeable plaintiffs. Further, the majority (Cardozo) is that the duty extends only to plaintiffs within the foreseeable zone of the danger. Conversely, the minority (Andrews) is that the duty extends to all plaintiffs. Also important to the first element is what the duty actually is: the standard of care. There are many different standards of care that will be discussed below.

Whether a duty and standard of care is breached is fact specific, but can look to industry custom, regulations or health codes, and any other relevant information.

For causation, plaintiff must establish both actual and proximate cause. Actual cause is causation in fact; but for the defendant's actions, the plaintiff's injury would not have occurred. Proximate cause is a limitation on liability, and says that the injury must be foreseeable; the defendant is generally liable for all harm that is the normal incident of and within the increased risk of his conduct.

Lastly is damages, which must be to the person or property.

The analysis for these elements in part differs depending on who the action is against; thus, they will be discussed accordingly.

(1) Action for Negligence against the Caterer: The action can be based on negligence or arguably negligence per se; both will be analyzed below.

(i) Duty to Patron: Here, Caterer is working in a restaurant and cooking food that is to be served to customers. Thus, he owes a duty to all customers because they are foreseeable plaintiffs and within the zone of danger of his negligent conduct, meaning they will eat his food and get sick. The standard of care here could be a variety of things, but regardless of which the court chooses, the Caterer will have breached it.

 The first possible standard of care is the common law one: a person must act as an ordinary, reasonable, and prudent person would act in the same circumstances as the defendant. Such a standard does not take into account the mental capacity of the defendant, but may take into account any physical incapacities. The court may also take into account any expertise or knowledge that he has, such as being a caterer or chef. This is the most likely standard of care.

 The second possible standard of care is that of a professional: which requires that a person act with the knowledge and skill of a professional in good standing in his community. It is arguable that a caterer is a professional, but less likely.

 The last standard of care is Negligence Per Se which will be discussed with breach.

(ii) Breach of the Duty:
 Looking to the first possible standard of care, Caterer clearly breached it by not checking the temperature on the oven despite the warning from both the clearly present Notification which he observed and from the waiter's comment to him. A reasonable and prudent person would have done so in light of these circumstances, and even without such obvious notifications, it would also be required because it is generally common knowledge that undercooked chicken is dangerous.

 The second possible standard of care will have a similar outcome. This is an even higher standard of care, which the Caterer cannot meet. If a caterer or chef is considered a professional, then a reasonable and prudent caterer or chef would surely check the temperature and have the right temperature for cooking meats, especially chicken.

Lastly is negligence per se. Negligence per se is that the generally common law standard of care may be replaced when there is a government regulation, statute, or as is here a health notification, that imposes a criminal penalty, which includes a fine. If negligence per se is established, then it is conclusively presumed that the negligence elements of duty and breach are satisfied. To establish negligence per se, the regulation must be violated without excuse, the plaintiff must have been within the protected class meaning the type of person the regulation sought to protect, and lastly that the plaintiff suffered the type of injury that the regulation sought to avoid. The first issue with negligence per se is whether the Notice constitutes a regulation or statute imposing a criminal penalty. It may not and if it doesn't, then negligence per se does not apply. It is possible it will not because nothing in the facts shows there is a penalty for such a violation. Conversely, usually there are large fines for violating these health code notifications and so it may be ok. Thus, if it does satisfy the first element of negligence per se, it has obviously been violated because caterer cooked the chicken at 250 instead of 350 degrees. Further, there was no evidence of an excuse the 250 degree-cooking. Next plaintiff was clearly in the protected class the notice sought to protect; the notice sought to protect patrons from getting sick. Lastly, plaintiff suffered the type of injury the notification sought to avoid; food poisoning. Thus, it is very possible that the court will determine negligence per se applies. But regardless of the outcome with negligence per se, it will likely be held that Caterer breached his duty under the common law negligence standard of care.

(iii) Causation: actual cause and proximate cause. Looking first to actual cause, defendant's negligent act of undercooking the meat was the cause in fact for plaintiff's injury. But for the undercooking of the meat, plaintiff would not have gotten food poisoning. Secondly, is proximate cause. Defendant's act directly proximately caused plaintiff's injury because it was foreseeable that serving undercooked meat to a patron would make the patron sick. Thus, the causation element is satisfied.

(iv) Damages: damages will be clearly established because plaintiff suffered food poisoning as a result of his negligence.

Thus, it is likely that the Patron would succeed in his action for negligence against the Caterer.

(2) Action for Negligence against the Waiter: The patron may have a claim for negligence against the waiter as well, essentially because the waiter observed the caterer's undercooking and ended up serving the food without confirming with the caterer that his mistake had been remedied. Again, for the waiter to be liable, the patron will have to establish the four elements of negligence.

The first element of duty: The waiter likely owes a duty to the patron because the patron is a foreseeable plaintiff within the zone of danger for his act of possibly negligently serving undercooked meat. Further, the standard of care would likely be the common law standard of care because none of the other standards of care apply to a waiter, which is a non-professional. Thus, the standard of care is that of an ordinary, reasonable, and prudent person in the same circumstances as the waiter.

The second element of breach: It is arguable that the waiter breached his duty to the patron. One the one hand, a reasonable and prudent person, after observing that the oven was set too low and the hearing caterer's defensive response to his inquiry, would likely make sure after the order was completed that the owner had remedied his mistake and changed the temperature of the oven because a reasonable person would be aware of the dangers of serving undercooked chicken to a patron. A reasonable person might also notify the owner of the carelessness to which the caterer is cooking, especially since he will only be working there one day. Conversely, a reasonable and prudent person might assume that after warning the caterer of the oven-temperature error, that he would simply correct his error and that the caterer's snappy response merely derived from his embarrassment at undercooking a chicken. Thus, the court could really go either way in determining whether the duty was breached, but it seems more likely that the court would determine that it was breached.

The third element is causation: The actual cause will be satisfied because but-for the waiter serving the undercooked chicken, the patron would not have gotten sick. However, the proximate cause is more difficult to establish, but still likely will be. Although the waiter did not undercook the meat, his negligence (if it is found) contributed to the patron's injury. The waiter's act is likely said to be an intervening force or negligent act. The waiter's failure to ensure that the chicken was cooked properly contributed to the patron's injury and was within the normal incidents of and the increased risk of his conduct. Thus, while more difficult because it is a more tenuous cause, it is likely the court will determine this element to be satisfied.

The fourth element is damages: this will be satisfied because the patron suffered food poisoning.

Thus, it is likely the patron will succeed against the waiter for a negligence claim.

(3) Action for Negligence against Owner: The patron may have a view actions for negligence against the owner of the restaurant. The first being an ordinary negligence claim under vicarious liability. The second being direct negligence for the negligent hiring and or supervision of the employee. All will be discussed.

The owner can be liable for the negligence of his employees, and even possibly the acts of independent contractors, under vicarious liability. Vicarious liability says that the master may be liable if the acts of his servant were within the course of employment. Generally, an owner or master will not be liable for the intentional torts of his servants or employees, unless the intentional tort was natural in the nature of the job, performed at the request of the master, or for the master's benefit. Here, there is nothing to suggest an intentional tort, but rather negligence.

Above, it has been established that the caterer was negligent, and thus, his negligence may be attributed to the owner. The first important determination is whether or not the caterer is an employee or an independent contractor. This is important because the vicarious liability of the owner differs depending on this. Generally, to determine whether someone is an employee or independent contractor, the courts look to several factors: degree of skill required in the job, who provided the tools and facilities, duration of the relationship, did principal control the means of performing the task, was there a distinct business, etc. Applying those facts to this case, it would appear that the Caterer was more likely an independent contractor. The reason being that the employment was only for one day, it was because the owner's normal cook was out for the day, the owner did not operate that much control over the caterer, the caterer had his own distinct business, and the caterer brought his own knives. Thus, if the caterer is determined to be an independent contractor of the owner, the owner generally is not liable unless one of the two exceptions apply.

An owner is liable for the acts of his independent contractor in two situations: (i) when the independent contractor is performing an inherently dangerous task and (ii) when because of public policy, the principal's duties are non-delegable. The latter of the two exceptions likely applies here. Public policy requires that an owner of an establishment that invites and charges members of the public for certain services must reasonably maintain their premises and ensure they are safe. Thus, just because the caterer was an independent contractor, does not mean that the owner could delegate the duty to maintain his restaurant and make it safe. Thus, the owner will likely be vicariously liable for the negligence of the caterer.

It should be noted, that if for some reason the court finds that the caterer was actually an employee of the owner because he was using the owner's kitchen and cooking the owner's menu items, then the owner would also be liable because the negligence occurred within the scope of his employment: it occurred while cooking on the job for a patron of the restaurant.

The owner may also be vicariously liable for the negligence of the waiter (if the waiter is found to have been negligent), because the waiter is an employee and the negligence occurred while acting within the scope of his employment.

The patron could also sue the owner for his Direct Negligence. Even if the owner is not vicariously liable, he can be directly liable for his own negligence. All persons are generally personally liable for their own negligence. Here, the direct negligence would arise from the owner's negligent hiring and arguably negligent supervision of the caterer. The owner owes a duty to his patrons to employ persons that are qualified and will perform the job responsibly. The patron will argue that the owner negligently hired the caterer because he gave him the job when the caterer was only an acquaintance. Further, the owner did not check the Caterer's references or ask around, which a reasonable person would have done; and if such acts had been done, he would have learned that the Caterer's business had once been shut down by the health department for violations. It was the owner's negligent hiring that was the actual, and very likely, the proximate cause of the plaintiff's injuries. Thus, the patron will likely succeed in this direct negligence claim against the owner.

The patron could also sue the owner for his Direct Negligence for negligent supervision of his employees. This is less probable because although the facts do not state that the owner inspected the caterer's work and watched him perform, it is not unreasonable for an owner to not check the every move of a caterer or chef. That being especially true when the caterer is performing such a standard task as cooking chicken. Thus, while the owner owed a duty to supervise, it was likely not breached. The duty here takes on the standard of care required for invitees: which is that the owner must make reasonable inspections to discover all non-obvious and dangerous artificial and natural conditions. That standard of care does not cleanly apply here, and even if it does, it is not apparent that it has been breached. Further, his failure to supervise may not be the proximate cause, because of the caterer's intervening act that was likely not the normal incidents of a failure to adequately supervise. Thus, it is likely the patron will lose on this claim.